Keys to Living a Fruit - Filled Life

Nine Keys That Will Unlock the Door to Success in Your Life

By

Miranda Burnette

Keys to Success Publishing, LLC

Atlanta, GA

Unless otherwise indicated, all Scripture quotations are taken from the *King James Version* (KJV) of the Bible.
Scripture quotations marked (AMPC) are taken from the *Amplified Bible Classic Edition.*
Scripture quotations marked (NIV) are taken from the *Holy Bible, New International Version.*
Scripture quotations marked (MSG) are taken from the *Message Bible.*
Scripture quotations marked (NKJV) are taken from the *New King James Version* of the Bible.
Scripture quotations marked (NLT) are taken from the *Holy Bible, New Living Translation.*
Scripture quotations marked (NASB) are taken from the *New American Standard Bible.*

Keys to Living a Fruit-Filled Life: Nine Keys That Will Unlock the Door to Success in Your Life

ISBN: 978-0692993552

P. O. Box 314
Clarkdale, GA 30111

www.mirandaburnetteministries.org

Keys to Success Publishing
Atlanta, GA 30127

Cover Design by Jackie Moore

DEDICATION

I dedicate this book to the students of Keys to Success Academy, Inc. I appreciate each of them very much, and I am thankful for all of their dedication and support. May God bless each of you in all of your endeavors as you strive to be the leaders God has called you to be.

CONTENTS

INTRODUCTION

This book, *Keys to Living a Fruit-Filled Life,* will address the keys to a happy, productive, fulfilling life. These keys will unlock the door to the successful life you have always wanted. By *fruit,* I don't mean apples, bananas, or oranges. I mean the fruit of the Holy Spirit mentioned in the Bible in the Book of Galatians Chapter 5 verses 22-23.

The fruit of the Spirit is love, joy, peace, patience, kindness, goodness, humility, faithfulness, and self-control. With the fruit of the Spirit operating in your life, you would be happier, easier to get along with, less stressed, a great influence in the lives of others, and you would be more successful.

If you are a Christian, you have the seed of the fruit of the Spirit already on the inside of you. According to Romans 5:5, God poured His love into you. The Amplified translation of this verse says,

"Such hope never disappoints or deludes or shames us, for God's love has been poured out in our hearts through the Holy Spirit Who has been given to us.

All you have to do is to water those seeds with the Word of God and start exercising them in order for them to develop in your life. As the fruit of the Spirit develops in your life, you will manifest the character of God because the fruit of the Spirit equals the qualities of God. You may have been waiting on God to do great things in your life, promote you or to give you the desires of your heart, such as a large business or ministry. However, God is waiting on you to grow up and mature, so you will be able to handle those things. Are you prepared for what God has prepared for you?

The development of the fruit of the Spirit in your life represents your spiritual maturity. Develop the fruit of the Spirit in your life so that you will be mature enough to handle the blessings God has in store for you. Then you will be on your way to being all He has created you to be. This book has all of the keys you need to be prepared when opportunity knocks.

Success always comes when preparation meets opportunity.

__Henry Hartman

So begin to read about and explore the fruit of the Spirit, and learn how this fruit can influence your life and equip you to go out and make a difference in the lives of others in a great way. Get ready to have success in your life, achieve your goals, and make such an impact on others that they will never be the same. May God bless you to mature and grow in Him daily, and bear abundant fruit as you live *A Fruit-Filled Life!*

Miranda Burnette

CHAPTER 1

THE FRUIT-FILLED LIFE

Everything was created to give forth fruit. In the Book of Genesis, in the very first chapter of the Bible, God told Adam and Eve to be fruitful and multiply.

Genesis 1:28 (KJV) says, And God blessed them, and God said unto them, be fruitful, and multiply, and replenish the earth, and subdue it: and have dominion over the fish of the sea, and over the fowl of the air, and over every living thing that moveth upon the earth.

The word *fruitful* means producing good results, beneficial, profitable, or producing an abundant growth *(Dictionary.com)*. Synonyms for *fruitful* are worthwhile, successful, rewarding, useful, plenteous and fertile *(Dictionary.com)*.

If you are fruitful, you should be able to bring forth something that can be plucked. When the Bible speaks of fruitful, it means to be fertile. Fertile means abundantly productive or capable of growth or development as seeds or eggs *(Dictionary.com)*. Fertile also means capable of reproducing. Synonyms for fertile are abundant, productive, bearing, and fruitful *(Dictionary.com)*.

Land or soil can be fertile or fruitful. If a piece of land or soil is fertile, that means it is bearing, producing, or capable of producing vegetation, crops, etc., *(Dictionary.com)*.

In the same way, your life can be fruitful. God wants our lives to produce fruit that can be plucked. Then our fruit will benefit the lives of others.

If your life is bringing forth fruit that can be seen and plucked by others to meet their needs, then your life is fruitful, just like God intended for it to be. Is your life fruitful? Let's look at *Galatians 5:22-23 (AMPC)*, and find out.

But the fruit of the [Holy] Spirit [the work which His presence within accomplishes] is love, joy, (gladness) peace, patience (an even temper, forbearance), kindness, goodness (benevolence), faithfulness, gentleness (meekness, humility), self-control (self-restraint, continence). Against such there is no law [that can bring a charge].

According to *Dictionary.com*, fruit is anything produced or accruing, a product, result, return, profit, or an effort. Synonyms for the word *fruit* are development, produce, or outgrowth *(Dictionary.com)*. There are nine different fruits listed in Galatians chapter 5. Actually, there is one fruit with nine different ingredients. Notice that the word *fruit* is *singular,* yet there are *nine things* listed in Galatians 5:22-23.

There is only one fruit of the Spirit. In Greek the word for *fruit* is *karpos* and it is in the singular.

The word *fruit* is *singular* and indicates that all the *fruit* exists as a *single unit* like a bunch of grapes rather than many different pieces of fruit, and that all are important to all believers. All together, they are the *fruit* (singular) of the spirit. In other words, all the nine things are really one thing that you have because the Holy Spirit indwells you, if you are a Christian. You just need to develop them.

The Holy Spirit produces all nine of these things in us simultaneously and constantly. We cannot choose which fruit we want. The fruit of the Spirit *is* love. Love is *the* fruit of the Spirit. All of the other fruit comes out of love.

All of the other fruit issues from love and actually are a form of love. All of the others are facets of love. If you are loving, then will you not have joy? If you are loving, will you not also have peace? If you are loving, will you not also be patient, kind, good, faithful, gentle (humble), and self-controlled? Love is like the tree that bears the fruit of joy, peace, patience, kindness, goodness faithfulness, gentleness (humility), and self-control. The nine things are all characteristics of the one fruit – love.

THE NINE FRUITS ARE DIVIDED INTO THREE CATEGORIES

THE FIRST THREE ARE INWARD AND COME FROM GOD

1. Love: God's love has been poured out in our hearts.
2. Joy: The unspeakable joy of the Lord is our strength.
3. Peace: Jesus said, "Peace I leave with you." We can have peace without understanding in the midst of storms in our lives.

When you praise God, you start releasing this love, joy, and peace, which are already in your born-again spirit.

THE SECOND THREE CONCERN EACH CHRISTIAN'S RELATIONSHIPS WITH OTHERS

3

1. Patience: Are you patient with others?
2. Kindness: Do you show kindness to others when they are not kind to you?
3. Goodness: Are you good to other people?

THE FINAL THREE ARE MORE GENERAL TRAITS IN A CHRISTIAN'S LIFE

1. Faithfulness: Are you a faithful person?
2. Gentleness *(meekness, humility):* Are you gentle, meek, and humble?
3. Self-control: Do you use self-control, self-disciple, and self-restraint when you need to?

The fruit of the Spirit is about inner character, not outward conformity. The fruit of the Spirit is developed gradually and is conditional in growth. Fruit takes time to grow and requires care and cultivation. Developing the fruit of the Spirit takes prayer, obedience to God's Word and practice.

If you examine yourself, you might notice that some of the fruit, the individual aspects of love, are not all that well developed. You might be kind and good, but need to work on your patience. You might have great joy and peace, but need work on self-control and gentleness. None of us is perfect. We all have areas of improvement. The Spirit produces the fruit. It is our job to live in harmony with the Spirit.

We have to cooperate with the Spirit in bearing this fruit. As I said, there is one fruit of the Spirit, but it manifests itself in nine ways. Individuals who have the Spirit have all nine of these attributes in them, whether they ever manifest them or not. You can think of the fruit of the Spirit as an orange with nine sections. All nine qualities of the fruit of the Spirit are seen in the character of God.

THE FRUIT OF THE SPIRIT EQUALS THE QUALITIES OF GOD

1. Love: "God is love." *(1 John 4:8, ESV)*
2. Joy: "He will rejoice over you with gladness." *(Zephaniah 3:17, ESV)*
3. Peace: "May the God of peace be with you all." *(Romans 15:33, ESV)*
4. Patience (longsuffering): "The Lord is longsuffering and abundant in mercy…" *(Numbers 14:18, NKJV)*
5. Kindness: "But when the kindness of God our Savior and his love for mankind appeared…"*(Titus 3:4, NASB)*
6. Goodness: "Oh, how great is Your goodness…" *(Psalm 31:19, NKJV)*
7. Faithfulness: "Great is Your faithfulness." *(Laminations 3:23, NIV)*
8. Gentleness (humility): "Your gentleness has made me great." *(Corinthians 10:1, NIV)*
9. Self-control: In regard to sin, "God cannot be tempted by evil." *(James 1:13)* In regard to His emotions, "So the Lord relented from the harm which He said he would do to His people." *(Exodus 32:14, NIV)*

This is not the fruit we bear; it is the fruit the Spirit bears in us. When the Spirit lives within us, all these characteristics (in varying degrees) are in our lives. When the Holy Spirit is in us, we have what He has. When you accepted Jesus as your Lord and Savior, a seed of His Spirit was planted in you. It is to be expressed in your thoughts, attitudes, the words you speak, and the way you interact with people. The fruit of the Spirit is in seed form and is waiting to be watered with God's Word. It is also waiting for your willingness to let God cultivate it in your life. When you get born-again, God himself comes and reside on the inside of you. When you receive the Holy Spirit, then the Holy Spirit's fruit comes inside of you also. The Holy Spirit's dominate fruit is love and all of the love is on the inside of you.

According to *Romans 5:5 (AMPC), Such hope never disappoints or deludes or shames us for God's love has been poured out in our hearts through the Holy Spirit who has been given to us.* You might not perceive it but according to God's Word, it is there. The fruit of the Spirit is already in those of us who are Christians.

BELIEVERS AS TREES

The Bible says that we (believers) are like trees, fruit bearing trees of righteousness, branches that are full of fruit.

Psalm 92:12 (AMPC) says, "The [uncompromisingly] righteous shall flourish like the palm tree [be long-lived, stately, upright, useful, and fruitful]; they shall grow like a cedar in Lebanon [majestic, stable, durable, and incorruptible."

Jeremiah 17:8 (AMPC) states, "For he shall be like a tree planted by the waters that spreads out its roots by the river; and it shall not see and fear when heat comes; but its leaf shall be green. It shall not be anxious and full of care in the year of drought, nor shall it cease yielding fruit."

Psalm 1:1-3 (AMPC) tells us how to bear fruit at the right time. It says,

"BLESSED, (HAPPY, fortunate, prosperous, and enviable) is the man who walks and lives not in the counsel of the ungodly [following their advice, their plans and purpose], nor stands [submissive and inactive] in the path where sinners walk, nor sits down [to relax and rest] where the scornful] and the mockers] gather. But his delight and desire are

in the law of the Lord, and on His law (the precepts, the instructions, the teachings of God) he habitually meditates (ponders and studies) by day and by night, And he shall be like a tree firmly planted [and tended] by the streams of water, ready to bring forth its fruit in its season; its leaf also shall not fade or wither; and everything he does shall prosper [and come to maturity]."

PEOPLE NEED LOVE

Can someone pluck some love off the branches of your tree? Sometimes your *patience* is a tremendous blessing to someone. For example, if someone owes you some money and he needs more time to pay you, can he pluck some fruit of patience from your branches?

Showing *kindness* to someone just might make that person's day. Are your branches full of kindness? The same is true with *gentleness*, which is being humble. Don't be proud and act as if you are better than someone else is. Do you have enough gentleness to last all day?

When you are *peaceful* in a bad situation, when others see that, it makes them have hope that they can do the same thing. Can peace be found on your tree? That is the same way with *joy*. When others see that, you have joy when you should be sad, they are encouraged and realize that if God can do it for you, He can do it for them too.

If you are *faithful* on your job, you are a great benefit to your boss and to yourself. The Lord promotes people who are faithful. We can show *goodness* by giving someone in need material items that we own. If you use *self-control* in your home and don't get mad and out of control with your family, you are producing something that will be of use to your family.

We have to make sure we do what Psalm 1:1-3 says about meditating on the Word of God day and night in order to produce fruit in our lives.

These verses let us know that if we meditate on the Word of God day and night, we will be like trees planted by the streams of water. Firmly planted means stable. If we are firmly planted when the storms of life come our way, we don't lose control and get into emotional turmoil. We are stable. We have self-control. We don't let our emotions control us. We control our emotions.

GIFTS ARE GIVEN, BUT FRUIT IS DEVELOPED

Many people have gifts that will get them somewhere, but they don't have enough character to keep them there once they get there. The fruit will keep you where your gifts and talents take you. We have to be mature enough to handle what God gives us. You might be waiting on your blessings, but God is waiting, like a parent, until you are mature enough to handle them. For example, you wouldn't give your ten year old the keys to your car and let him or her drive it, would you?

The development of the fruit of the Spirit operating in our lives is linked to our spiritual maturity. That is another reason why developing the fruit of the Spirit in our lives is so important. As we know, the fruit of the Spirit is the character of God. A display of the fruit of the Spirit, the nature of God, is a display of the character of Jesus Christ.

According to *2 Corinthians 5:20 (AMPC)*, we are God's ambassadors and He is making his appeal to humankind through us as believers in Jesus Christ. This verse states,

"So we are Christ's ambassadors, God making His appeal as it were through us. We [as Christ's personal representatives] beg you for His sake to lay hold of the divine favor [now offered you] and be reconciled to God.

It is important to God that we develop the qualities of His nature. It is God's will for each of us to have more love, joy, peace, patience, kindness, goodness, faithfulness, humility and self-control in our lives. Gifts come as seeds and mature when nurtured like everything else.

The gifts will function to a degree without fruit and for a certain period of time, but without fruit they will never mature. It is time to concentrate on what is important. Pray for, seek, and cultivate the gifts, but make the fruit a priority. Through developing the character qualities of the fruit of the Spirit, we are able to move into the blessed life God has in store for us.

YOU WILL KNOW THEM BY THEIR FRUIT

Either make the tree sound (healthy and good), and its fruit sound (healthy and good), or make the tree rotten (diseased and bad), and its fruit rotten (diseased and bad); for the tree is known and recognized and judged by its fruit (Matthew 12:33, AMPC).

Jesus said…The tree is known, recognized, and judged by its fruit. A good tree can be recognized by its fruit, and that applies to us as much as it does to trees. We are known by our fruit.

John 13:35 (AMPC), tells us that we are known to be Jesus' followers by our love for one another,

By this shall all [men] know that you are My disciples, if you love one another if you keep on showing love among yourselves.

Jesus is known by our fruit when others see the character qualities of God in our lives. This is a very big responsibility and we should take it very seriously. If you listen to what people say, you can tell a lot about them.

9

We as Christians must develop fruit in our lives by practicing and exercising the fruit in our lives every chance we get. Just as muscles are developed when we exercise them, the fruit of the Spirit will gradually be developed in our lives. Therefore, start today showing love, kindness, gentleness (humility), self-control and the other fruit in your life, and become like a tree that is planted by the streams of water. Just as it is very important for each of us to develop fruit in our lives, it is also important for us to be aware of the fruit or lack of fruit that is in the lives of others of whom we associate.

We need to know how to decide whether to be in relationship with someone who may be trying to deceive us. Remember, a tree is known by its fruit. If the fruit is bad, even though you might not see it from the outside, the tree is also bad. We need to look at their attitude and character because what is in that person will eventually come out. If someone is not honest and constantly don't keep their word, they have a character problem.

As leaders, when you are looking for someone to hire to fulfill a position, the first thing you need to look for is character. The other qualities are important too, but character is of the upmost importance because you are as good as the people who are around you and under you. You should hire for character, and train for skill. In this case and in other cases such as, choosing the right friends, business partners etc., you should become a 'fruit inspector.'

FRUIT INSPECTORS

Matthew 7:20 (KJV) says, "Wherefore by their fruits ye shall know them."

We have to be fruit inspectors. The way that you can tell whether a person is genuine or not is by the fruit they produce. This fruit is referring to their lifestyle. Jesus said in Matthew 7:18 (NIV),

"A good tree cannot bear bad fruit, and a bad tree cannot bear good fruit." Jesus pointed out that you don't get bad fruit from a good tree and you don't get good fruit from a bad tree.

Many people say one thing; but their actions say something else. Their actions speak so loudly that you really can't hear what they are saying. Again, if you are in doubt about whether a person is genuine or not, look at the fruit they are producing. Also, make sure that the fruit that comes from your own life is good. Make sure you are making a positive impact on people's lives. Be aware, people are looking at you to see what kind of fruit you are producing too.

HOW DO WE PRODUCE GOOD FRUIT?

If you want to bear good fruit, submit and obey God and His Word. When we honor God and do good things, we are bearing good fruit.

For the fruit of the Spirit is in all goodness and righteousness and truth (Ephesians 5:9, KJV).

The fruit of the Spirit is borne in all goodness, righteousness and truth. Ungodliness hinders the growth of the fruit of the spirit in our lives. Just as seeds cannot grow without light, so the darkness of ungodliness in our lives limits the production of the fruit of the Spirt.

If we cultivate a life of hatred, the fruit of love will not manifest. If we are truly born again, that love is present in our spirits, but it cannot flow while we are operating in hatred. In John 15, Jesus spoke of bearing fruit and declared, "Without Me you can do nothing."

Jesus said in John 15:4-5 (NIV),

"Remain in me, as I also remain in you. No branch can bear fruit by itself; it must remain in the vine. Neither can you bear fruit unless you remain in me. I am the Vine; you are the branches. If you remain in me and I in you, you will bear much fruit; apart from me you can do nothing."

If we want the fruit of the Spirit to grow in us, we must align our lives to God and His Word. We can't obtain them by trying to get them without His help. The fruit spoken of in these verses is not produced by the *believer* but by the Holy Spirit as we live in union with Him. The Spirit produces these character traits of God in us. Remember, this fruit is the product of the Holy Spirit, not our effort.

But whoever is united with the Lord is one with him in spirit.

1 Corinthians 6:17, NIV

Then this fruit of the Spirit is also, what our born-again spirit produces. Our spirit always has these attributes regardless of what we feel. Our part is to yield and trust God and God's part is to produce the fruit in our lives. Therefore, as you go out today, let your light shine by expressing the fruit of the Spirit in your life everywhere you go, and allow God to use you to be a powerful influence in the lives of others and make such an impact in their lives that they will never be the same.

DISCUSSION QUESTIONS

1. Name the nine fruits of the Spirit.
2. In the Book of Genesis, what did God tell Adam and Eve to do?
3. What does the word fruitful mean?
4. The nine fruits are divided into three categories. What are the

three categories?

5. The fruit of the Spirit equals the _____ of God.

6. What is the Holy Spirit's dominate fruit?

7. What does Psal*m 1:1-3* let us know about producing fruit in our lives?

8. Gifts are given to each of us, but fruit is _____.

9. In *Matthew 12:33,* what did Jesus say the tree is known, recognized, and judged by?

10. Complete the following scripture passage:

John 15:4-5 (NIV),

4 Remain in me, as I also remain in you. No branch can bear _____ by itself; it must remain in the vine. Neither can you bear _____ unless you remain in me.

5 "I am the _____; you are the _____. If you remain in me and I in you, you will bear much _____; apart from me you can do nothing.

CHAPTER 2

LOVE ONE ANOTHER

The fruit of love can be seen in how we treat people. If you are a Christian, God has commanded you to bear the fruit of love.

John 13:34 (AMPC) says, "I give you a new commandment: that you should love one another. Just as I have loved you, so you too should love one another."

As stated in chapter one, love is *the* fruit of the Spirit. All of the other fruit comes from love. All of the other fruit issues from love and actually are a form of love. Love ties all the other fruit together. You can't have self-control, gentleness (humility), patience, joy, goodness, peace, faithfulness, and kindness if love is not involved. When we really understand love and walk in it, then all of the other fruits are naturally present. The fruit of love helps all the other fruit grow.

WHAT IS LOVE?

The original Greek word for love is *Agape (ag-ah-pay)* and it means a caring and seeking for the highest good of another person without motive for personal gain. Love forms the foundation for all the other fruit listed in the Book of Galatians.

Galatians 5:22-23 (NIV) says, But the fruit of the spirit is love, joy, peace, forbearance (patience), kindness, goodness, faithfulness, gentleness and self-control.

Against such things there is no law. Love seeks the good of the one to whom it is directed.

GOD'S DEFINITION OF LOVE

God has clearly explained what love is in 1 Corinthians 13:4-7 (NIV):

"Love is patient, love is kind. It does not envy, it does not boast, it is not proud. It does not dishonor others, it is not self-seeking, it is not easily angered, it keeps no record of wrongs. Love does not delight in evil but rejoices with the truth. It always protects, always trusts, always hopes, and always perseveres."

THERE ARE FOUR DIFFERENT WORDS IN GREEK FOR LOVE

Eros is the attraction men and women have for one another. *Storge* is the affection parents and children have for each other. *Phileo* is the love one has for his friends. *Agape* is the highest form of love; it seeks the highest good of others regardless of relationship or circumstance.

Agape is the love which is produced by the Spirit in a Christian. *Agape* love is the kind of love that will really make a difference in our lives, in our relationships, in our marriages, and on our jobs. It is a higher quality of love. It is love on a higher level. Love is God's character and nature. God proved his love for us in that while we were still sinners Christ died for us.

Romans 5:8 (AMPC) says, "But God shows and clearly proves his [own] love for us by the fact that while we were still sinners, Christ (the Messiah, the Anointed One) died for us."

How Does the World Know That We Are Disciples of Christ?

By this shall all [men] know that you are My disciples, if you love one another [if you keep on showing love among yourselves].

John 13:35, AMPC.

We can cultivate all the fruit by focusing on love. If God's love is the basis for our actions, we are representing him well because 1 John 4:8 tells us that God is love. Love is the most important fruit because God is love. Love is not just something God does, but it is who He is. He can't help but love us because He is love. God loves us because he wants to – not because we deserve it.

Love Is Not Selfish

2 Timothy 3:1-2 (ESV) states, "But understand this, that in the last days there will come times of difficulty. For people will be lovers of self, lovers of money, proud, arrogant, abusive, disobedient to their parents, ungrateful, unholy,

Love is the opposite of selfishness. Don't let selfishness win the war. When you let love conquer selfishness, selfishness will be defeated. As we continue to walk in love, the fruit of love will develop and mature. God is the source of love. Over time as we study and learn God's Word and His ways, we grow the fruit of love in our lives. As we seek God and submit ourselves to Him, and allow Him to take control of different areas of our lives, the fruit of love will grow because God is love.

LOVE IS A CHOICE.

It is something you can choose to put on. Colossians 3:12-14 (NIV) tells us to, clothe ourselves with the love of God.

"Therefore, as God's chosen people, holy and dearly loved, clothe yourselves with compassion, kindness, humility, gentleness and patience. Bear with each other and forgive one another if any of you have a grievance against someone. Forgive as the Lord forgave you. And over all these virtues put on love, which binds them all together in perfect unity."

When you clothe yourself with the love of God, you clothe yourself with kindness, humility (gentleness), patience, and forgiveness. Love helps you to cultivate all the elements of the fruit of the Spirit. Love is the root of character.

As long as the fruit is attached to its root, it flourishes. Fruit that is detached from its root will eventually spoil. Let God's love flow through you. Receive God's love, love yourself, love God, and let him flow out of you to other people.

Love is not a feeling. Many people think that love is some kind of emotion, a certain type of physical feeling that you have. We are always searching for that feeling because some of us think that feeling is all love is. We talk about falling in love and falling out of love, which means either we feel emotions or we don't feel emotions.

Love is more than a feeling. Operating in love is a choice, not a feeling. Your power is in the love of God. Is the fruit of love growing in your life? Begin to develop the fruit of love in your life today, and see

17

your life blossom and flourish as you spread the fruit of love everywhere you go.

DISCUSSION QUESTIONS

1. How can the fruit of love be seen?
2. If you are a Christian, what have you been commanded by God to do?
3. What helps all of the other fruit of the Spirit grow in our lives?
4. What is love?
5. What is God's definition of love and where in the Bible can it be found?
6. What are the four different words in Greek for love?
7. According to Romans 5:8 (AMPC), how did God show and prove His love for us?
8. How does the world know that we are Disciples of Christ?
9. Complete the following verse of scripture.

   1 John 4:8 (KJV) – He that loveth not knoweth not God; for

   _____.

10. Who is the Source of love?

CHAPTER 3

NO JOY - NO STRENGTH

1 Peter 1:8 (AMPC), "Without having seen Him, you love Him; though you do not [even] now see Him, you believe in Him and exult and thrill with inexpressible and glorious (triumphant heavenly) joy."

The joy that I are talking about is unspeakable joy, a joy that is inexpressible.

WHAT IS JOY?

Joy is a shout, a proclamation that can manifest in singing. Joy is defined as a triumph, a cheerful and calm delight. Joy is a gladness of heart, a rapture in the soul that goes far beyond happiness.

The original Greek word for joy is *chara (khar-ah)* and means the feeling of gladness based on the love, grace, blessings, promises and nearness of God that belong to those who believe in Christ. It means cheerfulness or to be exceedingly joyful. j*oy* and *grace* come from the same root in Greek. Joy is an inner rejoicing that abides despite outer circumstances.

This characteristic has very little to do with happiness and can exist in times of unhappiness. It is a deep and nourishing satisfaction that continues even when a life situation seems empty and unsatisfying. When the fruit of joy is operating in our lives, our relationship with God through Christ remains even in the deserts and valleys of living.

The Bible uses the word *joy* and *joyful* 250 times. The word *rejoice* appears 200 times. Joy is not totally based on our circumstances. For example, if your circumstances are down, then your joy is down. If your circumstances are up then your joy is up. If you let your circumstances control your life, you will be like a yo-yo, up and down, up and down. Happiness is based on what is happening, but joy is not. Joy is like a deep well inside of us.

NO JOY – NO STRENGTH

Nehemiah 8:10 tells us that the joy of the Lord is our strength.

Nehemiah 8:10 (AMPC) states, "Then [Ezra] told them, go your way, eat the fat, drink the sweet drinks, and send portions to him for whom nothing is prepared; for this day is holy to our lord. And be not grieved and depressed, for the joy of the lord is your strength and stronghold."

A stronghold is a place where you can be protected from enemies. Remember, the battle starts in your mind, even the battle for your joy. Your *peace* and *joy* are connected. When you lose your peace, you lose your joy. When you lose your joy, you lose your strength, because the joy of the Lord is your strength.

Psalm 16:11 (AMP) says, "You will show me the path of life; in Your presence is fullness of joy, at Your right hand there are pleasures forevermore."

Psalm 118:24 (NLT) says, "This is the day the Lord has made. We will rejoice and be glad in it."

Let the fruit of joy mature in your life.

Philippians 4:4 (NIV) tells us to, "Rejoice in the Lord always. I will say it again: rejoice."

Rejoicing is something we do. Joy is something we have. Notice that Paul instructs us to rejoice in the Lord because our joy is in the Lord. That means that our joy is in our born-again spirits. Joy doesn't come from the outside in response to circumstances. Joy comes from the inside and is a fruit of the Spirit. Our outward circumstances may sometimes be against us, but inward joy can always be ours because we are in the Lord. We must think on good things to stay joyful.

Philippians 4:8 (NIV) states, "Finally, brothers and sisters, whatever is true, whatever is noble, whatever is right, whatever is pure, whatever is lovely, whatever is admirable—if anything is excellent or praiseworthy—think about such things;"

We always have joy, but we must choose to rejoice. Our joy is a witness to others. The Bible says, "We are the salt of the earth and the light of the world."

BELIEVERS ARE SALT AND LIGHT

Matthew 5:13-16 (NIV) states, "You are the salt of the earth. But if the salt loses its saltiness, how can it be made salty again? It is no longer good for anything, except to be thrown out and trampled underfoot. "You are the light of the world. A town built on a hill cannot be hidden. Neither do people light a lamp and put it under a bowl.

21

Instead they put it on its stand, and it gives light to everyone in the house. In the same way, let your light shine before others, that they may see your good deeds and glorify your father in heaven."

Your disposition of always being joyful and happy no matter what is going on, could be one of the main things that could draw others into a relationship with the Lord. You can't do that if you are a depressed, sad, and discouraged Christian. Our lights should shine through our attitudes and our smiles. Just imagine! You could win someone to the Lord, and he could become a Christian and have eternal life, all because of the joy of the Lord in your life.

Philippians 3:1 (KJV) says, "Finally, my brethren, rejoice in the Lord. To write the same things to you, to me indeed is not grievous, but for you it is safe."

The words *joy* and *rejoice* were used sixteen times in this short letter. This letter is one of Paul's most joyous epistles, even though it was written while he was in prison. The Bible clearly teaches us that our joy is found in Christ and not in our circumstances. The fruit of joy begins as a seed, and it must be developed. Developing the fruit of joy takes time and practice. It is just like developing your physical muscles.

The development of your physical muscles doesn't happen overnight. Nor will the fruit of joy be developed in your life overnight. You may not feel like exercising the fruit of joy. You may have difficulties developing this character building exercise. Your fruit of joy may be squeezed as you are learning, but this is a normal part of developing your fruit and it is working your spiritual muscles. Sometimes it is difficult for us to develop our fruit, but with practice and God's help, we can.

John 15:1-2 (NIV) states, "I am the true vine, and my Father is the gardener. He cuts off every branch in me that bears no fruit, while every branch that does bear fruit he prunes so that it will be even more fruitful."

John 15:4-5 (NIV) states, "Remain in me, as I also remain in you. No branch can bear fruit by itself; it must remain in the vine. Neither can you bear fruit unless you remain in me. "I am the vine; you are the branches. If you remain in me and I in you, you will bear much fruit; apart from me you can do nothing.

Jesus is the vine. We cannot bear excellent fruit unless we dwell in Him. Our fruit matures and ripens as we stay on the vine, no matter what happens. Fruit picked too early is green, hard, immature, not fully developed, tasteless, and not very pleasant.

JOY IS A DECISION

David said, "I will rejoice in the Lord."

Psalm 35:9 (NLT), "Then I will rejoice in the Lord. I will be glad because he rescues me."

Joy is a decision. You can look at the problem, the disaster, the lack, the pain, the past, the mistake, or you can fix your focus on the Lord and stay joyful. The choice is yours. It is your decision.

Psalm 32:11 (NLT) says, "So rejoice in the Lord and be glad, all you who obey him! Shout for joy, all you whose hearts are pure!"

Emotions cannot be chosen. No one can tell you to feel happy if you are not happy. Joy is more than an emotion. Joy is also an attitude. You can choose to be joyful regardless of your circumstances. We can have joy in spite of our circumstances. God wants His people to be joyful. As Christians, we ought to be the most joyful people in the world because

23

we have hope.

Hope in the future will give us joy in the present. Something about joy many people don't understand is this: "People, who have joy, also have problems but because they know the truth of God's Word, it allows them to have joy in spite of their problems." We can be joyful in spite of our problems because we know that God is with us.

Isaiah 43:2 (NIV) says, "When you pass through the waters, I will be with you; and when you pass through the rivers, they will not sweep over you. When you walk through the fire, you will not be burned; the flames will not set you ablaze".

We can also be joyful in spite of our problems because we know that God will help us.

Psalm 43:5 (NIV) says, "Why, my soul, are you downcast? Why so disturbed within me? Put your hope in God, for I will yet praise him. My Savior and my God."

It is not your problem that is the problem; it is the way you see your problem that is the problem. When you are going through a hard time and you are confused, you can have joy. You can have joy during financial difficulty, physical difficulty, job difficulty, and relationship difficulty. You can have joy in your darkest moments, when you understand what Romans 8:28 (NIV) means:

"And we know that in all things God works for the good of those who love him, who have been called according to his purpose." "

Paul is actually saying that people who have joy have the knowledge and understanding that God is in control. Do you realize the amount of joy we would experience in our lives if we knew God was in total control of everything that happens to us and that everything had a purpose? God's purpose is for our good, our growth, and our spiritual development.

JOY AND HAPPINESS ARE NOT THE SAME

There is a big difference between joy and happiness. We cannot be happy without being joyful but we can be joyful without being happy. Solomon a very wise man said in Proverbs 17:22 (AMPC),

"A happy heart is good medicine and a cheerful mind works healing, but a broken spirit dries up the bones."

Therefore, by having a good attitude, being happy and of good cheer, we are taking the medicine we need to produce health and healing in our bodies. That is so powerful! On the other hand, when we have a bad attitude and we are discontent and unhappy all of the time, our bodies become unhealthy and we bring sickness and disease into our lives. So stay calm, be happy, and of good cheer.

Proverbs 15:13 (AMPC) says, "A glad heart makes a cheerful countenance, but by sorrow of heart the spirit is broken."

There is a direct link between our emotions and our physical health. This verse clearly states, the condition of the heart makes our countenance cheerful. Although we don't always feel like laughter, laughter is good for us. Laughter brings health and healing. We usually laugh because something makes us happy, but we can always use some joy.

THE DIFFERENCE BETWEEN HAPPINESS AND JOY

Happiness is external. Joy is internal. Happiness is based on feelings.

Joy is based on knowledge. Happiness depends on what happens to us. Joy depends on who lives within us. Happiness is temporary. Joy is permanent. Happiness depends on outward circumstances. Joy depends on inward character. Happiness is based on chance. Joy is based on choice.

The word *happiness* comes from the old English word *happ*, which literally means *chance*. This word suggests that if things happen the way we want them to happen, then we are happy, but if they don't happen the way we want, we are unhappy.

JOY IS POWERFUL

Remember, joy gives us strength to go through the storms of life. Joy is medicine for our wounded heart. Joy helps our light shine everywhere we go so our God can be glorified. Joy strengthens us for the battles in life. An attitude of joy gives us hope for the future. Don't let anything or anyone steal your joy, because the joy of the Lord is your strength.

DISCUSSION QUESTIONS

1. What is joy?
2. True or False: Joy is based on our circumstances.
3. Nehemiah 8:10 tells us that the joy of the Lord is our

    _____.
4. True or False: We must think on good things to stay joyful.
5. In Paul's letter to the Philippians, how many times were the words *joy* and *rejoice* used?
6. Where was Paul when he wrote the epistle of Philippians?
7. What is the difference between joy and happiness?
8. Complete the following verse of scripture:

Proverbs 17:22 (AMPC), A happy heart is good _____ and a cheerful mind works healing, but a broken spirit dries up the bones.

9. Complete the following verse of scripture:
    Romans 8:28 (NIV), And we know that in all things God works for the good of those who love him, who have been called

    _____.

10. Fill in the blank.

    Just by having a good attitude and being of good cheer, we bring _____ and _____ to our bodies.

CHAPTER 4

PEACE IN THE MIDST OF THE STORM

Jesus told his disciples in John 14:27 (AMPC), "Peace I leave with you; my [own] peace I now give and bequeath to you. Not as the world gives do I give to you. Do not let your hearts be troubled, neither let them be afraid. [Stop allowing yourselves to be agitated and disturbed; and do not permit yourselves to be fearful and intimidated and cowardly and unsettled.]"

Webster's Dictionary defines peace as a freedom from disquieting or oppressive thoughts or emotions. Peace comes from a Greek word, which means tranquility of mind. The original Greek word for peace is *eirene* and means the quietness of heart and mind based on the knowledge that all is well between the believer and his or her heavenly Father.

It is an inner quietness and trust in God's sovereignty and justice, even in the face of adverse circumstances. This is a profound agreement with the truth that God, not we, remains in charge of the universe.

The Hebrew word for peace is *shalom* and it indicates the idea of soundness of health—physically, mentally, emotionally, and spiritually. The Hebrew *shalom* is a wish for the well-being of another. *Shalom* means order and well-being. It means you have a sense of security, a sense of direction, a sense of the presence of God in the midst of tension, turmoil, hostility, and battle.

The peace that God promises you and me is not a peace absent of trouble. What he promises is to find us in the midst of our trouble, our difficulty, our dark days, and walk into our lives and speak peace to our spirit, even while everything around us is unraveling and coming undone. God promises that peace. Grace and peace was a common greeting in Paul's letters

Peace is a fruit of the Spirit, (Galatians 5:22-23). Therefore, as a Christian, you always have peace in your born-again spirit. You may not always feel peace because you are not always living out of your spirit. We can allow our emotions or thinking to control us, but peace is always present on the inside of us. All we have to do is turn off the things that dominate us from the outside and follow the peace that is in our spirit.

The word *bequeath* in this verse is a term used in the execution of wills. When people die, they usually bequeath, or *will* their possessions, especially things that are valuable, to the people they love who are left behind. In this passage, Jesus was going away. When He passed from this world to go to be seated at the right hand of His Father in heaven, He wanted to leave us something. Therefore, He left us his peace.

It doesn't matter what is going on around us, if we walk in the spirit and stand on the Word of God, we can have peace in troubled times. Our society defines peace as an absence of trouble. In other words, when things are good on the outside, we have peace.

Peace is not the absence of problems, but the presence of God in the midst of our problems. Jesus will bring us peace even in the midst of trials. Naturally, it's impossible to have peace while we are in the midst of trials. Supernaturally, we can be filled with peace despite what is going on around us. We can have the peace of God that passes all understanding. With God, peace is an inside job. We are changed from the inside out.

As previously stated, peace comes from the Hebrew word *shalom* which means wholeness and completion-nothing missing, nothing lacking. This is the peace spoken of in Isaiah 26:3 (NKJV):

"You will keep him in perfect peace, Whose mind is stayed on You,
Because he trusts in You."

WE KEEP OUR MINDS ON HIM IN THE FOLLOWING WAYS:

1. Praising Him
2. Praying to Him
3. Casting our cares on Him
4. Trusting Him
5. Not listening to negative talk from negative people
6. Meditating on the Word of God
7. Thinking on good things
8. Speaking in agreement with God's Word (saying what the Word of God says about us)
9. Not getting entangled with other people's problems (Help but don't get too involved)
10. Thinking and speaking positively

Perfect peace can only come from a perfect God. The peace referred to in Isaiah 26:3 has a lot to do with focus. Focusing on circumstances will cause consistent anxiety because circumstances constantly change and often go beyond our control, but God never changes and nothing goes beyond his control.

While others are losing their heads, the only way we can keep our heads is by focusing on the mighty God who we serve who stays in control and will change our circumstances. God's peace comes as we focus on Him and His goodness. When our minds are filled with thoughts of Him, we experience a supernatural peace that supersedes any peace found in the world.

Don't let anyone or anything steal your peace, the peace that God has given you. Protect your peace. Learn to say no. Not every good thing is a God thing. This means that if God is not leading you to do some that someone is asking you to do, don't do it just because it is a good thing. God may have something better He wants you to do. It might be good, but is God telling you to do it? You might be getting into something that might steal your peace.

God doesn't want us to be overwhelmed or burden down with too many cares. Don't try to do everything, because you can't. Organize your life. Spend time with God. Keep your life and things in your life simple.

Rest in Jesus and don't take things too seriously. Do not be in such a hurry or too busy. Slow down! God is not in a hurry, and you should not be in a hurry either. Do things God's way. God's way is the best way. Receive God's peace. Be led by the Holy Spirit. Keep your eyes on the Lord. Don't let anything or anyone pressure you into doing more than you can do in peace. Use the wisdom of God.

Philippians 4:6-7 (AMPC), Do not fret or have any anxiety about anything, but in every circumstance and in everything, by prayer and petition (definite request), with thanksgiving, continue to make your wants known to God. And God's peace [shall be yours, that tranquil state of a soul assured of its salvation through Christ, and so fearing nothing from God and being content with its earthly lot of whatever sort that is, that peace which transcends all understanding shall garrison and mount guard over your hearts and minds in Christ Jesus.

You and I can never understand the peace of God. In other words, we can feel the peace of God without understanding it. Jesus gives us peace that surpasses all understanding. You will have peace beyond comprehension, when you have the peace of God. You may have trouble all around you and people can't understand why you still have peace. I have experienced this in my own life. You may have too. At one time in my life, I was facing all kinds of trials and troubles, but God gave me his peace. God's peace doesn't depend on circumstances. It was peace without understanding.

Relatives and people who were close to me, said they could not understand how I could act like nothing was wrong even though I was facing all types of turmoil. One relative said, "You act like you don't care." It wasn't that I didn't care, but I had casted my cares upon the Lord. The battle was too much for me, but it was not too much for God, and he worked it out beyond what I could ever imagine. I kept my eyes on the Lord. I stayed focused on Him.

Whatever we focus on, we magnify. When something is magnified, it becomes bigger. We need to focus on God and magnify Him not the problem. In the midst of trials and afflictions, we should magnify God by praising and glorifying Him. As we praise our great big God, our problems become smaller.

Get your mind and eyes on the Lord. Open your mouth, and begin to praise Him while He solves your problems and gives you the strength to go through whatever you are facing right now. We serve a great big God!

In whatever challenge you are facing right now, if God does not fix it, you can't do anything about it anyway. Therefore, you might as well praise Him while he works it all out for you. There is nothing too hard for our God. Don't keep looking at your circumstances. Look at God. Keep your eyes on the Lord. Look to Jesus!

The Lord doesn't want us to be anxious or worried about anything. Instead, He said to pray about them, and give God thanks, even before we see the answer. The devil is always trying to steal our peace. He knows that if he can steal our peace, he will also steal our joy. As mentioned in the previous chapter, we know that we need our joy because the joy of the Lord is our strength. If we don't have strength, it makes us vulnerable and weak. Peace is powerful! This is a saying I heard in church many years ago:

"No peace – No power"

"Little peace – Little power"

"Much peace – Much power"

Psalm 29:11 (NIV) says, "The Lord gives strength to his people; the Lord blesses his people with peace."

In 1 Peter 3:11, the Bible talks about three areas where we are to pursue peace—with God, with ourselves, and with others.

We are not to just hope for or wish for peace in these relationships, but we are to go after it with all our heart. If we don't have peace with God, we won't have peace with ourselves, and if we don't have peace with ourselves, we will never have peace with others.

1 Peter 3:10-11 (AMPC), For let him who wants to enjoy life and see good days [good—whether apparent or not] keep his tongue free from evil and his lips from guile (treachery, deceit). Let him turn away from wickedness and shun it, and let him do right. Let him search for peace (harmony; undisturbedness from fears, agitating passions, and moral

33

conflicts) and seek it eagerly. [Do not merely desire peaceful relations with God, with your fellowmen, and with yourself, but pursue, go after them!]

THREE KINDS OF PEACE

PEACE WITH GOD

This peace comes from knowing that one has a right relationship with the God of this universe.

Romans 5:1 (NIV) states, "Therefore, since we have been justified through faith, we have peace with God through our Lord Jesus Christ,"

This is eternal peace. When we talk about having peace with God, what we are really saying is that God, through his son, Jesus Christ, on a cross, has forgiven us of our sins and our heart no longer condemns us.

1 John 3:21 (NIV) states, "Dear friends, if our hearts do not condemn us, we have confidence before God.

This peace comes from knowing our sins are forgiven and Jesus Christ is our Savior. This peace comes from knowing that our names are written in the Lamb's Book of Life. It comes from knowing our God will never, never, as the Hebrew writer said, *"Forsake us or leave us."* This peace helps us understand that God is in control. Paul tells us that if we love God and are walking obediently in his plans, then everything that happens to us is for our ultimate good.

PEACE WITH YOURSELF

This is about having peace on the inside. This peace is an inside job.

This the inner tranquility that escapes most people today. You cannot be at true peace with others until you are at peace with yourself. This is internal peace.

Colossians 3:15 (NIV) states, "Let the peace of Christ rule in your hearts, since as members of one body you were called to peace. And be thankful."

Stop comparing yourself with other people. Stop determining your worth and value by how people have or are treating you. Listen to what God says about you in His Word, not what others say about you. Stop putting your confidence in "outward" things such as, looks, the kind of job you have, your level of education, gifts and talents, friends, car, and possessions.

Stop being a people pleaser. Let go of past mistakes and press toward the future God has for you. Stop letting other people run your life, and be led by the Holy Spirit.

PEACE WITH OTHERS

This is about having peace in relationships. This peace is necessary for relationships to flourish. This is external peace.

Romans 12:18 (NIV) states, "If it is possible, as far as it depends on you, live at peace with everyone."

The following list consists of ways we can enjoy peace with others.
- ✓ Get the strife out of your life.
- ✓ Stop letting your emotions rule you.
- ✓ Learn to keep quiet when God says to keep quiet.
- ✓ Keep your opinion to yourself.
- ✓ Don't try to control others.
- ✓ Respect other people's rights of individuality.

- ✓ Let people to be who they are
- ✓ Forgive those who hurt you.
- ✓ Don't be easily offended.
- ✓ Don't become angry every time you don't get your way.

FINDING GOD'S PEACE IN THE MIDST OF THE STORM

John 16:33 (NIV) tells us, "I have told you these things, so that in me you may have peace. In this world you will have trouble. But take heart! I have overcome the world."

Everyone goes through storms. When the storms of life come, how will you respond? Will you lose your peace, worry, and get anxious? The Bible says to be anxious for nothing.

Philippians 4:6 (NIV) tells us, "Do not be anxious about anything, but in every situation, by prayer and petition, with thanksgiving, present your requests to God."

There are many kinds of storms. You may be experiencing a financial storm. You may be in a difficult relationship at this time. Your health may not be in the best shape.

There may be problems on your job or you may need employment. It doesn't matter what type of storm you are going through right now. You can experience inner peace that isn't dependent on outer circumstances. What do we do when the storms come? How do we stand against them?

Matthew 7:24-27 (NIV) says, "Therefore everyone who hears these words of mine and puts them into practice is like a wise man who built his house on the rock. The rain came down, the streams rose, and the winds blew and beat against that house; yet it did not fall, because it had its foundation on the rock. But everyone who hears these words of mine and does not put them into practice is like a foolish man who built his house on sand. The rain came down, the streams rose, and the winds blew and beat against that house, and it fell with a great crash."

GOD IS OUR ROCK!

Isaiah 26:4 (AMPC) says, "So trust in the Lord (commit yourself to Him, lean on Him, hope confidently in Him) forever; for the Lord God is an everlasting Rock [the Rock of Ages]."

You can stand firm on the "Everlasting Rock," because He will never let you down. He is a solid foundation you can confidently stand on. Things around you may shake, but you will not fall. If the whole world around you is shaking, you can hold on to your Rock, the Lord Jesus Christ. God is your reliable source of supernatural peace.

WHAT TO DO WHEN THE STORMS COME

STAND ON THE WORD OF GOD

Sometimes people wonder, "Why should I spend so much time reading, studying, and meditating on God's Word?" This is why! When the storm comes; when discouragement, disappointment, despair, hurt, pain, and suffering is clouding your mind, those verses that you've hidden in your heart will start coming out of your mouth. In addition, God's Word will give you peace in the middle of the storm. Don't be moved by what you see with your natural eyes. Be moved by God's Word. Take the medicine of God's Word.

Matthew 14:28-30 (NIV) says, "Lord, if it's you," Peter replied, "tell me to come to you on the water." "Come," he said. Then Peter got down out of the boat, walked on the water and came toward Jesus. But when he saw the wind, he was afraid and, beginning to sink, cried out, "Lord, save me!"

Do you realize that when Peter stepped out on the water to walk toward Jesus, he wouldn't have started sinking if he had kept his eyes on the Lord? Nevertheless, what did he do? He let the circumstances around him, the wind rising, waves roaring, and the storm raging, cause fear to arise in his heart. Then he began to fear, he lost his peace. When he lost his peace, he started to sink.

The same thing is true in your life. When you keep your eyes focused on the Word of God, His Word will help you walk on top of the circumstances. However, if you begin to focus on your troubles and problems, you're going to sink.

Proverb 4:22 (NIV) says, "For they are life to those who find them and health to one's whole body."

The medicine of God's Word will heal your body. It will heal your emotions, it will heal your mind, it will heal and restore your relationships, it will heal you home, and it will heal your marriage. Moreover, when you take the medicine of God's Word, there will be no harmful side effects. You will just have God's perfect peace. Trust in the Lord and I acknowledge Him, lean and depend on God!

Proverbs 3:5-6 (NIV), Trust in the Lord with all your heart and lean not on your own understanding; In all your ways submit to Him, and he will make your paths straight.

HAVE FAITH IN GOD.

Mark 11:22-24 (NIV), "Have faith in God," Jesus answered. "Truly I tell you, if anyone says to this mountain, 'go, throw yourself into the sea,' and does not doubt in their heart but believes that what they say will happen, it will be done for them. Therefore I tell you, whatever you ask for in prayer, believe that you have received it, and it will be yours."

Speak the Word. Jesus spoke to the storm and it obeyed him. We can do the same thing.

Mark 4:39-41 (NIV), He got up, rebuked the wind and said to the waves, "Quiet! Be still!" Then the wind died down and it was completely calm. He said to his disciples, "Why are you so afraid? Do you still have no faith?" They were terrified and asked each other, "Who is this? Even the wind and the waves obey him!"

Cast your cares upon the Lord by faith.

1Peter 5:7 (NKJV) says, "Casting all your care upon him, for he cares for you."

The Bible says we are to cast all our cares upon God. What is a care? The Greek word translated *care* in 1 Peter 5:7 means to draw in different directions, distract, signifies 'that which causes this,' a care, especially an anxious care *(Vines Expository Dictionary).*

The whole purpose of care is to distract us from our fellowship with God. That is why it is so important for us to cast our care. Cares will blind us to God's peace. When we cast our cares upon the Lord, the peace will flow. If we want to experience the peace of God in our lives, we must learn to cast all our cares upon him and let them stay there. So let the peace of God flow in your life. Praise God while He calms the storms in your life and fight your battles. There is power in praising

God.

2 Chronicles 20:15 (NIV), He said: "Listen, King Jehoshaphat and all who live in Judah and Jerusalem! This is what the Lord says to you: 'do not be afraid or discouraged because of this vast army. For the battle is not yours, but God's."

2 Chronicles 20:22 (NIV) says, "As they began to sing and praise, the Lord set ambushes against the men of Ammon and Moab and mount Seir who were invading Judah, and they were defeated."

Praise stops the enemy in his tracks, and God begins to work. Praise opens up the door for God to work in our lives.

BE LED BY PEACE

Colossians 3:15 (AMPC) says, "And let the peace (soul harmony which comes) from Christ rule (act as umpire continually) in your hearts [deciding and settling with finality all questions that arise in your minds, in that peaceful state] to which as [members of Christ's] one body you were also called [to live]. And be thankful (appreciative), [giving praise to God always]."

LET PEACE RULE

The Greek word for *rule* comes from the root word from which we get our English word *umpire,* which means to govern or arbitrate. Govern means to rule over by right of authority *(Dictionary.com).* Synonyms for govern are, control and lead *(Dictionary.com).* Arbitrate means to decide between opposing or contending parties or sides *(Dictionary.com).* Synonyms for arbitrate are; determine, intervene, mediate, judge, decide, and umpire *(Dictionary.com).*

We can understand this in the same way we understand the function of an umpire in baseball. The umpire in a ball game decides if you are in or out of the game. Once the umpire makes the call, it is decided. His decision is final. In the same way, peace should be the umpire in your life that decides if a thing should be in your life or out. The peace of God should act just like an umpire in our hearts, deciding which opportunities we should act on and which ones we should let pass by. When you have a decision to make, whether big or small, be led by peace. You need to go in the direction you have the most peace.

Natural peace is only experienced in the absence of problems. God has given us his supernatural peace to enjoy. God's peace is independent of circumstances. Many people are looking for peace today in every place but the right place, which is in the Lord.

Some try to find peace in possessions, pleasure, or pills. They are turning to drugs and alcohol to help them find peace. They discover too late that drugs and alcohol can only give temporary peace, but only God can give us lasting peace, which only comes through Jesus Christ. You can have peace no matter what is happening on your job, in your home or in the world. Start today enjoying a life of peace by casting your cares upon the Lord and receiving His peace in your life.

DISCUSSION QUESTIONS

1. How does *Webster's Dictionary* define peace?
2. Peace comes from a Greek word, which means
   _____.
3. What is the Hebrew word for peace?
4. What does the word *Shalom* mean?
5. What does the verse of scripture, Isaiah 26:3 (NKJV) say about peace?
6. Name five ways we keep our minds on Him.

7. Complete the following statement: Whatever we focus on, we
   _____.

8. According to Psalm 29:11 (NIV), with what does God bless His people?

9. Name the three kinds of peace mentioned in this lesson.

10. According to Isaiah 26:4 (AMPC), the Lord God is an Everlasting _____.

CHAPTER 5

PUT ON PATIENCE

Very little in life has ever been accomplished without the fruit of patience. The best attributes in your life are developed through a long, tedious, and trying process. Your greatest accomplishment will be made over a long period of time.

The best things in life will take a long time. That is why it is so important for each of us to develop the fruit of patience in our lives. Patience is long-spirited, long-suffering with mildness, gentleness, moderation, and constancy. Patience is the ability to be slow to anger, rather than quick to anger.

Proverbs 16:32(AMPC) says, "He who is slow to anger is better than the mighty, he who rules his [own] spirit than he who takes a city."

This type of person is sometimes spoken of as "having a short temper." The Bible calls patience longsuffering.

WHAT IS LONGSUFFERING?

Longsuffering is the willingness to exercise patience, perseverance, and persistence in the pursuit of worthy goals. The original Greek word for long-suffering is *makrothymia (mak-roth-oo-mee'-ah)* from a combination of two Greek words: The word *makro,* which means "long or slow," and the word *thymia,* which means anger. Their combination literally means to be long-tempered. Longsuffering means endurance, fortitude, patience, being slow to anger or despair.

Fortitude means mental and emotional strength in facing adversity, danger, or temptation. Longsuffering is the very opposite of short-tempered. It is the forbearance which endures injuries and evil deeds without being provoked to anger or revenge. It is patiently putting up with people who continually irritate us.

Patience is to be constant and consistent or to be the same all of the time, no matter what is going on. Patience is not waiting; it is how we act while we are waiting. It is also our attitude while we are waiting. Waiting on the Lord is the hardest thing for most Christians to do.

However, it is during the waiting periods of our lives that the most powerful things are happening on the inside of us. Therefore, patience is not an ability to wait. Patience is a fruit of the Spirit that manifest while we are waiting.

James 1:3 (AMPC) tells us to "Be assured and understand that the trail and proving of your faith bring out endurance and steadfastness and patience."

W. E. Vines states, "Patience is a fruit of the Spirit that can only be developed by going through trials."

We can learn how to use hard times as an opportunity to develop our faith. You can use hard times as stepping stones in your spiritual development. If you form the habit of quitting when things get hard, you will always miss opportunities for growth. Conflict makes champions! Greatness just doesn't happen, you have to persevere through hard times and be an overcomer. When your faith is being tried, exercise patience.

James 1:4 (AMPC), But let endurance and steadfastness and patience have full play and do a thorough work, so that you may be [people] perfectly and fully developed [with no defects], lacking in nothing.

Vines also states that patience perfects Christian character. God will give us patience when we ask for it. Nevertheless, we have to realize that our answer requires us to be patient.

PUT ON PATIENCE

Colossians 3:12 (NIV), Therefore, as God's chosen people, holy and dearly loved, clothe yourselves with compassion, kindness, humility, gentleness and patience.

Patience is something we choose to do. Patience is a decision.

Ecclesiastes 7:8 (KJV) tells us, "Better is the end of a thing than the beginning thereof: and the patient in spirit is better than the proud in spirit."

We have to be patient when we are trying to make our dreams and visions come to past.

Habakkuk 2:3-4 (KJV), For the visions is yet for an appointed time, but at the end it shall speak, and not lie though it tarry, wait for it; because it will surely come, it will not tarry. Behold, his soul which is lifted up is not upright in him: but the just shall live by his faith.

Faith requires patience. Luke 8:15 AMPC tells us to bring forth fruit with patience.

Luke 8:15 (AMPC), But as for that [seed] in the good soil, these are [the people] who, hearing the Word, hold it fast in a just (noble, virtuous) and worthy heart, and steadily bring forth fruit with patience.

We can only bring forth fruit with patience. The growth of a seed is a process and takes time. It is the same with our Christian life. Growing in the Lord also takes time.

The Christian life is not like a hundred yard dash but rather a twenty-six mile marathon. It takes time to become a fruitful Christian. You can't microwave the fruit of patient. It is a process. God isn't interested in microwave Christians. He wants to put us in the crockpot, let us simmer, and bring out the best in us.

It takes patience to be a fruitful Christian. It takes diligence. It also takes the Word of God. In this entire parable about the seed, the Word of God produced the fruit. The ground just gave it a place to grow. If we would simply put God's Word in our hearts, protect it, and give it priority in our lives, the word will produce fruit.

1 Corinthians 13:4 tells us that love is patient. One of the greatest ways to show love to others is to be patient with them. We have to be patient with their weaknesses and their faults.

We have to be patient with the way they behave or the way they act. We have to be patient with the way they treat us. When it comes to being patient with others, remember God's patience with you. Christ died for us while we were unloving and unwilling.

If we are patient and persevere, we will be better off in the end. Our faith will develop in patience, and the results of that will be that we become perfect and complete, wanting nothing.

Hebrews 10:36 (AMPC) says, "For you have need of steadfast patience and endurance, so that you may perform and fully accomplish the will of God, and thus receive and carry away [and enjoy to the full] what is promised."

We first have to believe, then act, and then be patient before we receive the full manifestation of what we believe. Patience is simply faith over a prolonged period of time.

Luke 21:19 (KJV) says, "In your patience possess ye your souls.

The content of this statement is about persecution and the compensation for enduring it that we will receive in the resurrection. Therefore, the patience that Jesus was speaking of here is the calm assurance that God knows every hurt that we feel, and he will abundantly recompense us in the resurrection.

This knowledge enables us to dominate our emotions in the face of persecution, instead of allowing our emotions of fear dominate us. This is how we possess our souls. Be patient! Patience is something we become, not something we strive to do. To exercise patience, you must endure something.

For example:
- ➤ Sticking with something and not giving up
- ➤ Staying in a situation that is unpleasant
- ➤ Not giving up on difficult people, by praying for them, covering their faults with love, and forgiving them

IMPATIENT PEOPLE

Impatient people always try to avoid or to eliminate discomfort or suffering. Because of this, they never come to the end of things; Therefore, they never develop. You have to go through in order to get from the beginning to the end of a thing. In the process, you are developing your spiritual muscles and the fruit of the Spirit in your life.

You are developing the character of God. However, impatient people do not want to go through anything. Impatience causes stress in our lives, and stress can causes all kinds of sickness. Anger is the root of impatience. Uncontrolled anger is the foundation for impatience. Anger itself is not wrong.

Ephesians 4:26 (NIV) says, "In your anger do not sin": Do not let the sun go down while you are still angry,

However, when anger in itself is not controlled or disciplined, it begins to rage and go into all forms of impatience. That is where it becomes wrong. Remember patience is slow to anger.

Hebrews 12:1 (ASV), Therefore let us also, seeing we are compassed about with so great a cloud of witnesses, lay aside every weight, and the sin which doth so easily beset us, and let us run with patience the race that is set before us,

Be patient in running the appointed course of the race set before you. Enjoy the journey. Be patient and learn to wait well. Patience will perfect Christian character. When you are not patient, you are controlled by your circumstances, disappointments, and people.

PATIENTLY WAITING

The following are examples of men in the Bible who waited patiently:

1. God developed Moses to be a great leader for the children of Israel, on the backside of the desert for 40 years.
2. Joseph spent many years in prison as God developed him.
3. God developed David through the patience of having to spend years as a refugee in caves, even though he was really anointed to be king.

48

4. Abraham obtained the promise of God; his son, Isaac, after he had patiently endured. Abraham waited 25 years to receive the promise of God. Are you willing to wait that long?

Isaiah 40:31(ESV) says, "But they who wait for the lord shall renew their strength; they shall mount up with wings like eagles; they shall run and not be weary; they shall walk and not faint.

Waiting on the Lord requires trusting him.

Psalm 130:5 (NIV), I wait for the Lord, my whole being waits, and in his word I put my hope.

Waiting on the Lord is not for his benefit. Waiting on the Lord is good for us. Waiting on the Lord is for our benefit. Waiting on the Lord will do the following for us:

✓ Helps us trust Him more
✓ Builds hope
✓ Teaches us obedience
✓ Builds our faith
✓ Helps us rely on His strength and not our own strength

Psalm 40:1 (AMPC), I waited patiently and expectantly for the Lord; and He inclined to me and heard my cry.

Are you waiting on God today? Are you patiently enduring? Remember, patience is not only the ability to wait, but also the attitude you have while you are waiting!

DISCUSSION QUESTIONS

1. What is patience?
2. Complete the following scripture verse.

Proverbs 16:32 (AMPC), He who is slow to anger is better than the _____, he who rules his [own] spirit than he who takes a _____.

3. What does the *King James Version* and the *New King James Version* of the Bible call patience?
4. What is long-suffering?
5. What is the hardest thing for most of us to do as Christians?
6. What does James 1:3 (AMPC) tell us the trial and proving of our faith bring out?
7. Ecclesiastes 7:8 tells us that the patient in spirit is better than the _____.
8. Name two characteristics of being impatient.
9. Name four great men in the Bible who waited patiently on the Lord.
10. What are three benefits of waiting on the Lord?

CHAPTER 6

SIMPLE ACTS OF KINDNESS

The *King James Version* of the Bible translates the Greek word for kindness as *gentleness* but in 2 Corinthians 6:6 as *kindness*. The original Greek word for kindness is *chrestotes,* and means not wanting to hurt someone or give him or her pain. Kindness, gentleness, and meekness are very much alike. The original Greek word for gentleness is *chrestos (khrase-tos')* or *chrestotes (khray-stot' ace)* and means: gracious, kind, excellence in character or demeanor, goodness, or kindness. Kind means being considerate, helpful, mild, and gentle.

Ephesians 4:32 (NKJV) says, "And be kind to one another, tenderhearted, forgiving one another, even as God in Christ forgave you."

Kindness is the ability to care for each other in the practical details of life. Kindness *(Vines Expository Dictionary)* means goodness of heart. Mercy is kind and kindness is merciful. Mercy gives others blessings they don't deserve. Mercy withholds punishment. We are supposed to be kind to others even when they are not kind to us.

"Constant kindness can accomplish much. As the sun makes ice melt, kindness causes misunderstanding, mistrust, and hostility to evaporate." __Albert Schweitzer

Being kind to others is about relationships. Being kind to others opens up the door for great relationships. Having good relationships is very important if you want to have success in your life. Nothing else matters more than relationships in the end.

"You cannot do a kindness too soon, for you never know how soon it will be too late.' __Ralph Waldo Emerson

If your relationship with others is not right, then nothing is going to be right.

"Success in life + failure at relationships = failure."

The moment that you and I fail in our relationships, no matter how *successful* we have been, we truly are a failure.

"How far you go in life depends on your being tender with the young, compassionate with the aged, sympathetic with the striving, and tolerant of the weak and strong because in life you will have been all of these." __ George Washington Carver

There are rewards or benefits for being kind. The Bible promises us in Luke 6:35 AMPC that we will receive a reward from God after we have been kind to other people. Anyone can react with kindness to acts of kindness. The real test of your fruit of kindness is to respond with kindness to those who don't show kindness to you. It is one thing to be kind to those who like us and treat us nicely, but it is another thing to be kind to those who don't.

It is very important, not only to be kind with deed, but also with our words. Not only with what we say to others, but also how we say it. The power that comes from speaking a kind word to someone or writing a kind note to him or her cannot be measured. When we are kind and friendly to others, the Bible says we will have friends.

Proverbs 18:24 (NKJV), A man who has friends must himself be friendly, but there is a friend who sticks closer than a brother.

Many people want friends, but they are not friendly. This verse reveals to us the way to make friends. Don't be so concerned about your needs, but think about the needs of others and be a friend to them. This is sowing and reaping. If you want a friend, become a friend. Then others will become a friend to you.

Friendship isn't about what others can do for you, but about what you can do for others. You reap what you sow. Sow kindness and you will reap kindness.

Galatians 6:7 (NKJV) says, "Do not be deceived, God is not mocked; for whatever a man sows, that he will also reap."

The person who gives kindness always receives more kindness than he gives. If we are kind,

- ✓ We will have lasting relationships.
- ✓ We will have a happier marriage.
- ✓ We will have more joy.
- ✓ We will have more peace.
- ✓ We will be healthier.
- ✓ We will please God.

A key to building relationships that will last is kindness. Take an opportunity to be kind to someone today. Sow the fruit of kindness everywhere you go, by word or deed, and watch as God multiply that seed and you reap the harvest of kindness back into your own life.

Remember, we reap what we sow. Sow kindness and reap kindness!

DISCUSSION QUESTIONS

1. What is kindness?
2. Being kind to others is about _____.
3. Success in Life + Failure at Relationships = _____.
4. What are three benefits of being kind?
5. What did Ralph Waldo Emerson say about kindness?

CHAPTER 7

BEING GOOD AND DOING GOOD

The original Greek word for goodness is *agathosune (ag-ath-o-soo'-nay)* and means zeal for truth and righteousness and a hatred for evil. It can be expressed in acts of kindness or in rebuking and correcting evil. It is reaching out to do good to others, even if they don't deserve it. Goodness does not react to evil but absorbs the offense and responds with positive action.

Goodness means what is upright or righteous. It signifies not merely goodness as a quality; rather it is goodness in actions, goodness expressing itself in deeds. *(Vines Expository Dictionary)* Goodness according to *Noah Webster Dictionary* is the moral qualities, which constitute Christian excellence. God is good, and because God is good, goodness should be manifested in the lives of his children.

Psalm 34:8 (AMPC), O taste and see that the Lord [our God] is good! Blessed (happy, fortunate, to be envied) is the man who trusts and takes refuge in Him.

Psalm 27:13 (AMPC), [What, what would have become of me] had I not believed that I would see the Lord's goodness in the land of the living!

Psalm 25:8 (AMPC), good and upright is the Lord; therefore will He instruct sinners in [His] way.

God is good, even when our situations are not. God wants to be good to you.

Isaiah 30:18 (AMPC), And therefore the Lord [earnestly] waits [expecting, looking, and longing] to be gracious to you; and therefore he lifts Himself up, that He may have mercy on you and show loving-kindness to you. for the Lord is a God of justice. Blessed (happy, fortunate, to be envied) are all those who [earnestly] wait for Him, who expect and look and long for Him [for His victory, His favor, His love, His peace, His joy, and His matchless, unbroken companionship]!

God wants us to be good to other people. When we do good deeds for other people, we are expressing or showing goodness. Learning to be good to people, no matter how difficult it may seem, is a basic requirement of experiencing God's goodness in life. God wants us to be good. God wants us to let his character, which is good, be developed in us.

God wants us to display the fruit of goodness in our lives by being good to other people. God never asks us to do anything that he doesn't show us first. He never asks us to be merciful to anybody else without giving us mercy. God would never ask us to forgive people who hurt us if he was not willing to forgive us first.

Romans 2:4 (NKJV) says, "Or do you despise the riches of his goodness, forbearance, and longsuffering, not knowing that the goodness of God leads you to repentance?"

We need to be good to people because the Bible tells us the goodness of God leads men to repentance. You can win someone over quicker by being good to him or her than anything else.

1 Timothy 6:17-18 (AMPC), As for the rich in this world, charge them not to be proud and arrogant and contemptuous of others, nor to set their hopes on uncertain riches, but on God, who richly and ceaselessly provides us with everything for [our] enjoyment. [Charge them] to do good, to be rich in good works, to be liberal and generous of heart, ready to share [with others].

The Lord is telling us to do good works. God gives us money and things so we can use the money and things to be a blessing to people. It is by doing good that we allow the fruit of God's goodness to flow to us and through us.

Galatians 6:10 (NKJV) says, "Therefore, as we have opportunity, let us do good to all, especially to those who are of the household of faith."

One of the most practical things we can do with the fruit of goodness is say good things to people that build, edify, exhort, and encourage them.

Proverbs 15:23 (AMPC) says, "A man has joy in making an apt answer, and a word spoken at the right moment – how good it is!"

SIMPLE ACTS OF KINDNESS

Simple acts of kindness are a nice way to show goodness. One very simple act of kindness is to smile. Another simple act of kindness to show goodness is to do kind things for people. You can be kind and show goodness by giving when you see a need. You can be kind by giving someone a compliment.

You can show goodness and kindness by giving the clothes or other items you want to sell to someone in need instead of trying to get money for them. God can bless you beyond what you could ever get from trying to sell them to get money for them.

Acts 20:35 (NIV) states, "In everything I did, I showed you that by this kind of hard work we must help the weak, remembering the words the Lord Jesus himself said: 'It is more blessed to give than to receive.'"

Jesus lets us know in Luke 6:45 that goodness is more than what we know or what we do; it is a matter of who we are.

Luke 6:45 (NIV), A good man brings good things out of the good stored up in his heart, and an evil man brings evil things out of the evil stored up in his heart. For the mouth speaks what the heart is full of.

Goodness is being good and doing good. Goodness is a matter of the heart. It has a lot to do with your motive, the 'why' behind the 'what' you do. So keep this in mind, whatever good we do, must be from our hearts. God looks on the heart.

Goodness motivates a person to attempt to do what is best for another. John Wesley, a great preacher and the founder of Methodism, said he lived by one creed:

Do all the good you can,

By all the means you can,

In all the ways you can,

In all the places you can,

At all the times you can,

To all the people you can,

58

As long as ever you can.

That is an awesome way to live! Live the 'Good Life' by doing good and being good!

DISCUSSION QUESTIONS

1. What is goodness?
2. _____ is Good!
3. God wants to be good to _____.
4. According to Galatians 6:10 (NKJV), God wants us to do good to _____.
5. A simple act of kindness is a nice way to show goodness. Name three simple acts of kindness.

CHAPTER 8

POWER UNDER CONTROL

What is humility? Humility can be defined as the absence of pride or the opposite of pride. Humility according to *Webster* is freedom from pride and arrogance. It is a modest estimation of your own worth.

It is having a modest opinion of one's own importance or rank. Humble means low-lying or to stay under *(Vines Expository Dictionary)*. An example of humility is, being under authority.

1 Peter 5:6 says to, "Humble yourself under the mighty hand of God."

Humility also means meekness. The word meek means to be gentle and mild *(Vines)*. The original Greek word for meek is *praus (prah – ooce')* and means gentle, humble, and gentleness. The original Greek word for meekness is *prautes (prah – oo' – tace)* and means restraint coupled with strength and courage. It describes a person who can be angry when anger is needed and humbly submissive when submission is needed.

This meekness is associated with self-control. Meekness means power under control. The terms meekness and mildness, commonly used, suggest weakness, but meekness is not weakness. A meek man is a powerful man. Meekness, which is also (humility, gentleness) is one of the most difficult Christian attitudes to cultivate in our lives.

The word humility and meekness have a negative connotation for many people, but in the biblical context, meekness means gentleness, caring, and a lack of quarrelsomeness or argumentativeness. It is having a modest opinion or estimation of one's own importance or rank. Jesus was humble and gentle and yet, he was a powerful man.

Zechariah 9:9 (AMPC) says to, "Rejoice greatly, O Daughter of Zion! Short aloud, O Daughter of Jerusalem! Behold, your King comes to you; He is [uncompromisingly] just and having salvation [triumphant and victorious], patient, meek, lowly, and riding on a donkey, upon a colt, the foal of a donkey.

The meekness entrusted or committed to believers and manifested by the Lord is the fruit of power. Therefore, we have to realize that meekness is not weakness. It is strength under control. It is the balance of spirit that is neither elated nor cast down. The word meek refers to a kind gentle spirit.

PRIDE

Pride on the other hand, as I stated before, is the opposite of humility. Pride according to *Webster* is inordinate self-esteem, an unreasonable conceit of one's own superiority in talents, beauty, wealth, accomplishments, rank, or elevation in office. It manifests itself in high-minded airs, distance from others, and often abuse of others. It is disrespectful, rude treatment of others, elevation, or a lifting up. The *Amplified* Bible translates pride as puffed up. Pride means to lift yourself up. Humble means to lower yourself.

Proverbs 16:18 (AMPC) says, "Pride goes before destruction, and a haughty spirit before a fall."

God blesses the humble. He lifts up the humble. He promotes them.

Proverbs 15:33 (AMPC) says, "The reverent and worshipful fear of the Lord brings instruction in Wisdom, and humility comes before honor."

Pride destroys us, and humility promotes and blesses us. Proverbs speaks often of how wisdom brings a long life, riches, favor, and honor.

James 3:13 (AMPC) states, "Who is there among you who is wise and intelligent? Then let him by his noble living show forth his [good] works with the [unobtrusive] humility [which is the proper attribute] of true wisdom."

Pride is something God hates.

Proverbs 6:16-19 (KJV), These six things doth the Lord hate: yea, seven are an abomination unto him: A proud look, a lying tongue, and hands that shed innocent blood, An heart that deviseth wicked imaginations, feet that be swift in running to mischief, A false witness that speaketh lies, and he that soweth discord among brethren.

THESE SEVEN THINGS THE LORD HATES:

1. A proud look - A proud look is the spirit that makes one over estimate himself and under estimates others.
2. A lying tongue
3. A hand that sheds innocent blood
4. A heart that manufactures wicked thoughts and plans
5. Feet that are swift in running to evil

6. A false witness who breathes out lies
7. He who sows discord, such as, strife, disagreement, conflict, quarreling, and arguments among his brethren Strife and discord come from judgment and criticism, which comes from pride.

1 Peter 5:6 (NLT) says, "So humble yourselves under the mighty power of God, and at the right time he will lift you up in honor."

AFRAID OF WHAT PEOPLE THINK

When we are afraid of what people think, it is also pride. We want them to think well of us to the point we allow them to control us in order to have their acceptance. You might ask, "Isn't the fear of man rooted in insecurity?" Yes, the insecurity causes us to be so desperate to feel important that we will do almost anything to get it.

DON'T LET PRIDE HOLD YOUR BACK

God knows how to humble those who have lifted themselves up. We all have strengths and we all have weaknesses. Weaknesses make us lean on God and prevent us from being independent, which is another indicator of pride. Pride can hinder your ability to forgive someone or move past a painful chapter in your life.

Don't let pride hold you back. Let it go and let God! Humble yourself and let God work this prideful unforgiveness out of your life. God can also give you a great talent or gift, but if you haven't developed humility, it can cause you to fall. God blesses those who are humble.

Matthew 5:5 (NIV) states, "Blessed are the meek, for they will inherit the earth."

HUMBLE YOUR THINKING

Be careful about how you think. We must be so careful about our thoughts. Pride also has a lot to do with our thinking, not just the way we act. Pride starts in our very own private thought life. It starts in the judgmental thoughts that we have toward others. I wrote a book titled *Success Starts in Your Mind.*

Success actually does start in your mind, and so does humility. Pride also start in your mind in the form of judgmental thoughts of others and criticism. Don't think more highly of yourself than you ought to. Your talents and abilities are a gift from God, given by His grace.

Romans 12:3 (KJV) says, "For I say, through the grace given unto me, to every man that is among you, not to think of himself more highly than he ought to think; but to think soberly, according as God hath dealt to every man the measure of faith."

1 Corinthians 10:12 (AMPC), Therefore let anyone who thinks he stands [who feels sure that he has a steadfast mind and is standing firm], take heed lest he fall [into sin].

Anyone who thinks he stands should be careful lest he falls.

Galatians 6:3 (AMPC) says, "For if any person thinks himself to be somebody [too important to condescend to shoulder another's load] when he is nobody [of superiority except in his own estimation], he deceives and deludes and cheats himself."

Are we supposed to think badly of ourselves? No! This does not mean that you never do anything for yourself. It means keep a modest view of yourself and keep yourself excessively off your mind. A quote by C. S. Lewis states:

"Humility is not thinking less of yourself, but thinking of yourself

less."

Constantly comparing yourself with others is pride. Be careful about comparing yourself with others.

Galatians 6:4-5 (AMPC) says, "But let every person carefully scrutinize and examine and test his own conduct and his own work. He can then have the personal satisfaction and joy of doing something commendable [in itself alone] without [resorting to] boastful comparison with his neighbor. For every person will have to bear (be equal to understanding and calmly receive) his own [little] load [of oppressive faults]."

Be careful about boastful comparisons. Each person has faults.

AVOID THIS TYPE OF THINKING:

- ➤ I'm thinner than you are.
- ➤ You are overweight.
- ➤ You should control yourself.
- ➤ You're not very intelligent.
- ➤ It is hard for me to have a conversation with someone so far below my level.
- ➤ I have more money than you do.
- ➤ I got the promotion, I must be better at my job than you are.
- ➤ God is using me more than He is using you.

Remember; be careful when you think you stand lest you fall. Stop comparing yourself with other people. Comparing yourself with others can only make you feel inferior or superior. Neither one is pleasing to God. If we notice ourselves sometimes, many of the questions we ask other people are for comparison. We ask them questions because we want to make sure we're ahead of everyone else.

CHARACTERISTICS OF THE PROUD

1. Independent – They don't think they need anyone, and sometimes that includes the Lord.
2. Love titles – They like having a position or title. They are selfishly ambitious. They really want to get a head and make a name for themselves. They want to be someone important in life. They prefer leading not following.
3. Rebellious – They do the opposite of what they are told and they refuse to submit to authority.
4. Unteachable – They can't stand to be corrected or to look wrong.
5. Impatient – They have difficulty being kind to those who are slow or make mistakes.
6. Frequently give opinions – They think they know something about everything.
7. Interrupt others frequently – They have difficulty letting others talk and difficulty listening.
   They think what they have to say is much more important than what others have to say.
8. A Victim Mentality

PRIDE CAN ALSO SHOW UP IN OUR LIVES IN WAYS IN WHICH WE ARE NOT AWARE:

For example:
➢ Perfectionism
➢ An inability to trust God
➢ A need to control circumstances
➢ A desire to impress people
➢ Fear of what people will think

> Status seeking

PRIDE CAN DISGUISE ITSELF AS A FORM OF HUMILITY

For example:
> Worry
> Insecurity
> Self-loathing – If someone feels self-loathing, he feels great dislike and disgust for himself. Self-loathing refers to an extreme dislike of oneself or being angry with oneself. You shouldn't dislike yourself. You should love yourself, because God loves you.

Pride can crept into your attitude wearing the sheep's clothing of humility. So beware!

BE CAREFUL HOW YOU THINK ABOUT OTHERS

Each time we judge, it is a result of pride. Each time we criticize, it is a result of pride. Each time we show disrespect, it is the result of pride. Our actions originate in our thoughts, therefore, be careful what you think. Pride comes before destruction and prevents promotion in our lives. Pride will bring you down quickly.

Sometimes a person will have a right spirit, but then when God promotes them, they become a different person altogether. They begin to think that they are better than someone else. They may even start to mistreat other people. God is not pleased with this. Pride is all about '*I.*'

A PROUD PERSON'S MINDSET IS:

- I am smarter than you are.

- I am better than you are.
- I can do it better than you can.
- Your opinion doesn't matter.

An example of this can be found in Luke 18:9-14 in the parable of the Pharisee and the tax collector. Pride is a destroyer. One of the best ways to determine whether pride is an issue in your life is if you honestly think you don't have any pride. If that is the case, that is a clear indication you've got a problem with pride.

Spiritual pride is the worst of all. Spiritual pride is the one that Jesus dealt with concerning the Pharisees. Those of us who think we are better than other people spiritually, will have the benefit of God orchestrating our humility. Do you know how to be humbled? Be humiliated!

If you don't humble yourself, then God will humble you. When God humbles you, it could be very humiliating. You don't want God to humble you. Therefore, if he is dealing with you about humility, you had better humble yourself.

First, God might ask you to do something that you don't want to do. He may even ask you 2 or 3 times, but you may refuse to comply because you are too proud. Next, in order to help you, because He loves you, He may tell someone else to tell you, at that point it could be very embarrassing or humiliating for you to hear it from someone else who you did not want to know about it in the first place. This all could have been avoided if you had been obedient to God the first time.

The Bible says to humble yourself under the mighty hand of God. It is better for us to humble ourselves instead of God humbling us. If we don't humble ourselves, God will be obligated to humble us, Himself. It is a lot less painful or humiliating to do it ourselves.

We don't want God to have to humble us. Pride is probably one of the biggest problems we deal with. Take this simple test, to test your level of humility:

✓ Do you forgive others easily?

✓ Is it easy for you to receive correction?

✓ Are you too proud to ask for help when you need it?

✓ Are you touchy? Do you get your feelings hurt easily?

✓ Are you a judgmental person?

✓ Do you always have to have the last word?

✓ Are you patient and longsuffering with the weaknesses of others?

As you allow God to deal with the areas of pride in your life, you will open the door to a deeper level of God's power in your life. Remember, humility is not weakness. It is power under control.

So let us do as 1 Peter 5:6 tells us to do. Humble yourself therefore, under the mighty hand of God, that he may exalt (raise you up) in due time.

DISCUSSION QUESTIONS

1. What is humility?
2. Humility also means _____.
3. What does the word meek mean?
4. A meek man is a _____.
5. What is pride?
6. Fill in the blanks to complete the following scripture verse: *Proverbs 16:18 (AMPC), Pride goes before_____, and a _____ spirit before a _____.*
7. According to Proverbs 15:33, what comes before honor?
8. Name the seven things God hates that are in Proverbs 6:16-19 (KJV).
9. According to 1 Peter 5:6, why does God want us to humble ourselves under His mighty hand?

10. What are four ways pride can show up in our lives in which we are not aware?

CHAPTER 9

FAITHFUL IN LITTLE - FAITHFUL IN MUCH

The fruit of faithfulness is listed as faith in the *King James Version* of the Bible, but many Bible translations call this fruit faithfulness. In the original Greek, the word faith is *pistis (pis' – tis)* and means faithfulness. It means firm and unswerving loyalty and adherence to a person to whom one is united by promise, commitment, trustworthiness, and honesty. In order for faith to develop and grow properly, we must *water* it with the Word of God.

Romans 10:17 (NKJV), "So then faith comes by hearing, and hearing by the word of God."

THE REWARDS OF FAITHFULNESS

Be faithful over little things first and your reward shall come.

"If you are faithful in little things, you will be faithful in large ones.

But if you are dishonest in little things, You won't be honest with greater responsibilities." (Luke 16:10 NLT)

To be faithful means to be strict or thorough in the performance of duty. Faithful means being true to one's word, promises, or vows. It is being reliable, trusted, and believed. A faithful person is dependable, constant, steady, and enduring *(Dictionary.com).*

Faithfulness is sticking with something, doing it over and over and over again, even when you don't feel like it. You do it even when others ridicule you and say bad things about you. God is looking for a few faithful men and women. Are you faithful? It doesn't matter how gifted a person is, if he or she is not faithful.

We all want to be successful in life and reach our goals and realize our dreams; But the Bible lets us know in this verse that if we are faithful in little things, we will be faithful in larger ones. If you want to be a success in life, be faithful. Being faithful is a key to success in life.

You may be constantly praying and asking God for big things or about going to the next level on your job. However, God is waiting on you to be faithful where you are presently before he moves you up higher. Why should God give you more responsibilities when you are not handling what you have?

Some of you may be wondering why you are not moving forward to the next level in your career. You may feel like you are stuck. Take an inventory of your life. Are you faithful where you are? If you want to be used by God in a great way, be faithful. Remember this: God promotes faithful people.

Psalm 75:6-7 (KJV), "For promotion (success) cometh neither from the east, nor from the west, nor from the south. But God is the judge: He putteth down one, and setteth up another.

God promotes those who have proven themselves to be faithful. One thing you can be assured of is, when you are faithful to God to do whatever he has called you to do, when God is ready to promote you, no one will be able to hold you back.

So many people are looking for human promotion. You don't have to be concerned about whether or not your employer is unfairly not promoting you. Promotion comes from the Lord. When God gets ready to promote you, He will. No one can stop God. Man doesn't hold the key to our destiny, God does. Promotion doesn't come from man. Promotion comes from God.

Why does God want us to be faithful before he promotes us? Faithfulness is a fruit of the Spirit. The fruit of the Spirit represents the character of God. God wants to build good character in us. Being faithful builds good character. We can't get very far in life without having good character. He wants us to be like Him. He wants to prepare us for the greater things He has in store for us. If He gives you more when you are not ready for it, it could cause problems in your life. If you can't handle small things, you definitely can't handle bigger ones.

Start being faithful today, and see God move mightily in your life. Don't let a great opportunity pass by you. Be faithful where you are. Sticking with something is the way to grow.

Galatians 6:9 (KJV) says, "Let us not be weary in well doing; for in due season we shall reap, if we faint not."

Never give up! Be faithful because God is faithful.

AREAS IN WHICH WE SHOULD BE FAITHFUL

❖ WE SHOULD BE FAITHFUL TO GOD

We should be faithful in what God has called us to do. We should be faithful stewards over our gifts. We should be faithful over whatever God blesses us with by taking care of it and managing our finances properly. It is not how much you make, but what you do with it, and the number one thing we should do with our finances is to put God first.

Luke 16:11 (AMPC) announces, "Therefore if you have not been faithful in the [case of] unrighteous mammon (deceitful riches, money, possession), who will entrust to you the true riches?"

❖ WE SHOULD BE FAITHFUL TO OUR SPOUSE.

❖ WE SHOULD BE FAITHFUL TO OUR CHILDREN.

When it comes to being faithful to our children, we have to remember how faithful God is to us, his children.

❖ WE SHOULD BE FAITHFUL TO OUR EXTENDED FAMILY.

❖ WE SHOULD BE FAITHFUL TO OUR PARENTS.

❖ WE SHOULD BE A FAITHFUL FRIEND!

If your friend shares something with you, don't go and tell someone else. Be there for your friend in hard times as well as good times. Don't just be a fair weather friend.

Proverbs 27:6 (AMPC) reveals, "Faithful are the wounds of a friend, but the kisses of an enemy are lavish and deceitful."

Be honest with your friend. Tell them the truth even if they don't like it. The truth hurts, but it is good for you. Remember to tell the truth in love.

❖ WE SHOULD BE A FAITHFUL CITIZEN.

We need to pray for our leaders. We should not cheat on our taxes. We should not break the law. We should keep the law of the land.

Romans 13:2 (AMPC) states, "Therefore he who resists and sets himself up against the authorities resists what God has appointed and arranged [in divine order]. And those who resist will bring down judgment upon themselves [receiving the penalty due them]."

❖ WE SHOULD BE A FAITHFUL MEMBER OF OUR CHURCH:

We need to get in a good church, grow, and bloom where we are planted.

Psalm 92:13 (KJV) says, "Those that are planted in the house of the Lord shall flourish in the courts of our God."

❖ WE SHOULD BE FAITHFUL TO OUR WORD

Have you ever considered that your word is the only thing not worth giving unless you keep it? You are no more than your word.

Psalm 15:4 (AMPC) says, "In whose eyes a vile person is despised, but he who honors those who fear the Lord (who revere and worship Him); who swears to his own hurt and does not change."

The Bible says that a godly man will swear to his own hurt and change not, the word godly means like God. God will swear to his own hurt and change not. We want to be like God, so let's keep our word. Swearing to our own hurt and not changing is considered a godly characteristic. Keeping our word is the right thing to do even when it isn't something we want to do or even if it is not convenient.

❖ WE SHOULD BE FAITHFUL IN OUR WORK:

Ecclesiastes 9:10 (NIV) says, "Whatever your hand finds to do, do it with all your might, ... "

Be a faithful employee and do your best on your job. Do it as unto the Lord and not unto man.

Colossians 3:23 (KJV) states, "And whatsoever ye do, do it heartily, as to the Lord, and not unto men;"

Luke 16:12 (AMPC), "And if you have not proved faithful in that

which belongs to another [whether God or man], who will give you
that which is your own [that is, the true riches]?"

DISCUSSION QUESTIONS

1. What does faithfulness mean?
2. In order for our faith to develop and grow properly, what must we do?
3. According to Romans 10:17 (NKJV), how does faith come?
4. *Luke 16:10 (NLT) says. "If you are faithful in little things, you will be faithful in _____.*
5. According to Psalm 75:6-7, where does promotion come from?
6. When God is ready to promote you, will people be able to hold you back?
7. What does the fruit of the Spirit represent?
8. Fill in the blanks to complete Proverbs 27:6 (AMPC). *Faithful are the wounds of a _____, but the _____ of an_____ are lavish and deceitful.*
9. According to Colossians 3:23 (KJV), how should we do whatever we do on our jobs?
10. Name five areas in our lives where we should make sure we are faithful.

CHAPTER 10

VICTORY OVER YOURSELF

In the original Greek, temperance is *egkrateia (eng-krat'-i-ah)* and means self-control. Self-control means having control or mastery over one's own desires and passions. Self-control is restraint exercised over one's own impulses, emotions, or desires. It is self-discipline, self-restraint, willpower, and level headedness. Self-control means to be strong in a thing, and temperance in appetite or appetites.

It is moderation and avoiding extremes, within reasonable limits. It is being mild or calm. It is self-restraint in action, speech, etc. Self-control is the art of controlling oneself. D. L. Moody, a great evangelist of the last century was asked, "Of all the people you come in contact with, who gives you the most trouble?" He said, "D. L. Moody. I have the most trouble with myself."

God gives us the fruit of self-control so that we can discipline ourselves. Unless we discipline ourselves, we will never have the things we desire. Self-control helps us make ourselves do what we should do, so we can have what we want and be all we can be. It is impossible to show forth the other eight fruits of the Spirit unless we are exercising the fruit of self-control.

For example, How can we remain peaceful in trails unless we exercise self-control? How can we exercise patience when we are frustrated, unless we exercise self-control? How can we be kind to someone when we don't feel good ourselves, unless we are exercising self-control? How can we exercise humility when we are corrected, unless we operate in self-control?

1 Timothy 3:2 (MEV) says, "An overseer then must be blameless, the husband of one wife, sober, self-controlled, respectable, hospitable, able to teach;"

LEADERSHIP AND SELF-CONTROL

Leaders must be self-controlled. As a leader, the first person you lead is yourself! We should understand that leadership is a big commitment. We cannot just commit to being a leader, we must commit to live the lifestyle that must accompany leadership, and that takes self-control.

The day you become a leader, you lose the right to live selfishly. The day you became a leader, you lost the right to live an out of control lifestyle. If I live an out of control lifestyle, it doesn't just influence me; it influences the people that I am leading.

Leaders, if you want to live a life without self-control, stay a follower. If you want to be a leader, change people's lives, and show them how you walk through the trials and tribulations of life, you are going to have to exercise self-control, no doubt about it.

"He that would govern others first must govern himself."

__ Philip Massinger

Here's an important leadership principle:

"The higher you go, the fewer options you have in life!"

"The first victory that successful people ever achieve or win is the victory over themselves." __ John Maxwell

Proverbs 25:28 (NLT) states, "A person without self-control is like a city with broken-down walls."

We all know that when this verse was written, cities were safe only because of their walls. The Proverb writer is saying that the moment we lose self-control and self-discipline, we are like a city without any kind of protection. Anything that is uncontrolled can harm your relationships.

UNCONTROLLED ANGER CAN DESTROY RELATIONSHIPS.

Proverbs 29:11 (NLT) says, "Fools vent their anger, but the wise quietly hold it back."

OUT OF CONTROL SPENDING CAN HARM RELATIONSHIPS.

Proverbs 21:20 (NLT) says, 'The wise have wealth and luxury, but fools spend whatever they get."

DRINKING TOO MUCH (ALCOHOL THAT IS) CAN BRING DESTRUCTION TO RELATIONSHIPS!

Proverbs 23:29-30 (NLT), "Who has anguish? Who has sorrow? Who is always fighting? Who is always complaining? Who has unnecessary bruises? Who has bloodshot eyes? It is the one who spends long hours in the taverns, trying out new drinks.

OUT OF BALANCED AMBITION CAN HURT GOOD RELATIONSHIP.

Proverbs 23:4 (NLT) says, "Don't wear yourself out trying to get rich. Be wise enough to know when to quit."

Self-discipline is an important part of a person's character. It will give them success and help them reach the highest potential they can possibly reach.

"What we do upon some great occasion will probably depend upon what we already are. And what we are will be the result of previous years of self-discipline." __ H. B. London

What you are going to be tomorrow, you are becoming today. It is essential to begin developing self-discipline in a small way today in order to be disciplined in a big way tomorrow. How do you eat an elephant? You eat an elephant, one bite at a time!

How do you tackle the big issues in your life? You tackle them, one-step at a time. Start small. Do what you can do today. How do you become a great spiritual giant? You do it by spending a little time with God every day, and gradually increasing it.

Self-control is postponing the impulsive pleasures in order to have the important things you want in life. Self-control is about delaying gratification and disciplining yourself to wait for what you truly want. We can't control other people and we shouldn't, but we can and should control ourselves. Self-control is the difference between victory and defeat in the game of life. Self-control is a key factor in whether we will be successful or not be successful. Either you can control self, or self will control you.

Successful people control their time.

Successful people control their tongue.

Successful people discipline themselves to achieve their goals.

Successful people manage their emotions.

Successful people control anger.

Successful people manage their finances.

Successful people control themselves.

John Hancock field says,

"All worthwhile men have good thoughts, good ideas, and good intentions, but precious few of them ever translate those into action."

The best time to get self-control in your life is today, not tomorrow. If you have dreams, goals, and visions you want to see come to past, you are going to have to practice discipline and self-control, so start now developing the fruit of self-control in your life. You will be glad you did.

DISCUSSION QUESTIONS

1. What is the meaning of self-control?
2. Why is it so important for a leader to be self-controlled?
3. Complete the following statement:
   The day you become a leader, you lose the _____ to live _____.
4. Proverbs 25:28 (NLT) tells us that a person without self-control is like _____.
5. Anything that is uncontrolled can harm your relationships. Name three.
6. Complete the following statement:
   Self-control is the difference between _____ and _____ in the game of life.
7. What are four areas of life in which successful people control in order to be and keep being successful?
8. Complete this quote by John Hancock Field:

> *"All worthwhile men have good thoughts, good ideas, and good intentions, but precious few of them ever translate those into_____."*

9. How should you tackle the big issues in your life?
10. How do you become a great spiritual giant?

CONCLUSION

THE GOOD LIFE!

Now, you have all of the keys you need to live a successful, blessed, happy life that is full of love, joy, peace, patience, kindness, goodness, humility, faithfulness, and self-control. The Word of God is powerful, and as you apply it to your life, it will change you. You will begin to grow and mature. You will then have the strength you need to overcome the obstacles that have been holding you back from being all God created you to be. God wants you to be successful.

Joshua 1:8 states, This Book of the Law shall not depart out of your mouth, but you shall meditate on it day and night, that you may observe and do according to all that is written in it. For then you shall make your way prosperous, and then you shall deal wisely and have good success.

Developing the fruit of the Spirit in your life is one of the greatest things you can do for yourself and others in your life. It is time to grow up! So begin to take the steps you need to take to grow up into a tree that is flourishing and producing plump delicious fruit that others can pick that will be useful to their lives.

You have the God-given potential to be all you can be. Don't fall short of what God created you to be. If you will put into practice, the principles found in this book, your life will improve and you will influence the lives of others in a positive way.

God wants you to have an *abundant fruit-filled life,* a life with blessings overflowing. As believers, we know Jesus came for one purpose, so we could live the abundant life.

The thief comes only in order to steal and kill and destroy, I came that they may have and enjoy life, and have it in abundance (to the full, till it overflows).

__ John 10:10 (AMPC),

The thief's purpose is to steal, kill, and destroy. *In John 10:10 (NLT),* Jesus says, "My purpose is to give them a rich and satisfying life." This abundant life is the *ZOE* life of God that resides on the inside of a Christian, enabling him or her to live supernaturally while on the earth. The Greek word translated *life* in this verse is *ZOE. ZOE* is the God – kind of life, and means *"Life in the absolute sense,"* life as God has it (*Vine's Expository Dictionary*).

Everyone who is breathing has physical life, but only those who receive Jesus can experience life as God intended for it to be. Believers can release this supernatural *ZOE* life and enjoy it now! When we line our actions, thoughts, and emotions up with the instructions of God's Word, which is life *(ZOE in John 6:63)* then we will find this *ZOE* life manifest in our bodies and souls as well.

It is the Spirit Who gives life [He is the Life-giver]; the flesh conveys no benefit whatever [there is no profit in it]. The words (truth) that I have been speaking to you are spirit and life. __John 6:63 (AMPC)

Jesus came not only to save us from our sins, but also to give us this

ZOE or God-kind of life in abundance. While Jesus' mission included the offer of an eternity with God in heaven upon accepting Him, He also came to make available to us the very *life force* of God Himself. So, what is the connecting factor to living this abundant life the Bible promises? The answer is found in

Proverbs 4:20-22 (AMPC), which says, "My son, attend to my words; consent and submit to my sayings. Let them not depart from your sight; keep them in the center of your heart. For they are life to those who find them, healing and health to all their flesh."

We see where life is located—in the Word of God. The Words of God bring life to those who find them. The Word of God will also bring healing to your whole body.

When we pay close attention to the Word, and internalize it, abundant life will flow out of us. We must make a quality decision to commit to the Word and consistently obey it. That is the way we access the abundant life, or success in every area of life. We must be doers of the Word to get the results.

So, how do we attend to the Word of God? Well, the *definition of attend is "To direct and apply oneself to pay attention,"* according to W*ebster's Dictionary.* Every day, we must allow our time spent with the Word to be our priority.

On a practical level, attend means spending time reading the Bible before we step out of the house in the morning. It means being consistent in making confessions of faith during the day. It also means listening to the Word being taught regularly, and allowing God's way of doing things to be the basis for how we handle the situations we face throughout the day and in life in general. This is what it means to attend to the Word of God.

If we would begin to refocus our attention on God's Word, and commit to making it the centerpiece of our lives, we will begin to see some amazing things begin to happen in our circumstances. The Word contains the *life force* of God that has the ability to eradicate anything that does not line up with the blessing. Attend to it and you will see results.

God desires for everyone to have the *Good Life*. We can only have the *Good life* when we receive that *Good life* from the *Source of Life*. We can have life in Jesus Christ. The first step to that abundant blessed, prosperous life, full of joy and peace and other nourishing fruit is to get connected to the *Source of Life* and that is God through Jesus Christ.

Jesus came that we may have life and have it more abundantly. The life that Jesus came to give is often referred to as eternal life in the Bible. This life is *ZOE,* the God kind of life. God is full of *ZOE.* It is the nature of God. Everything God is comes because of *ZOE.* When you were saved, you received the nature of God into your spirit.

If you have not accepted Jesus as your personal Savior, now is the time to do so. Let's put first thing first. All you have to do is to ask Jesus to come into your heart by faith. You can pray this prayer:

Lord Jesus, I admit that I am a sinner. I repent, turn away from my sins. I ask you to forgive me for my sins, come into my life and heart, and take total control. In Jesus name, I pray. Amen!

The moment you were born-again, *ZOE,* or the very nature of God, moved inside your spirit. *ZOE* affects our development as Christians. You have just connected to the *Source of eternal life, ZOE,* the God-kind of life, abundant life, and a Spirit led life here on earth and in heaven. Welcome to *THE GOOD LIFE!*

Obeying Him is an important key to growing up spiritually and reaping the benefits of the life of God in you. Read and meditate on God's Word so your spirit can grow stronger.

Begin to develop the fruit of the Spirit God has placed inside of you and use those keys, love, joy, peace, patience, kindness, goodness, humility, faithfulness, and self-control, to open the door to *SUCCESS IN YOUR LIFE!*

ANSWERS

CHAPTER 1

THE FRUIT OF THE SPIRIT

1. The nine fruits of the Spirit are love, joy, peace, patience, kindness, goodness, humility, faithfulness, and self-control.
2. Be fruitful and multiply
3. Producing good results; beneficial; profitable; producing an abundant growth
4. The first three are inward and come from God—love, joy, and peace

   The second three concern each Christian's relationship with others—patience, kindness, and goodness

   The final three are more general traits in a Christian's life—faithfulness, humility, and self-Control
5. The fruit of the Spirit equals the <u>qualities</u> of God.
6. Love
7. These verses let us know that if we meditate on the Word of God day and night, we will be like a tree planted by the streams of water ready to bring forth its fruit in its season.

8. Gifts are given to each of us, but fruit is <u>developed.</u>
9. Fruit
10. *John 15:4-5 (NIV)*

   4 Remain in me, as I also remain in you. No branch can bear <u>fruit</u> by itself; it must remain in the Vine. Neither can you bear <u>fruit</u> unless you remain in me.

   5 "I am the <u>Vine</u>; you are the <u>branches.</u> If you remain in me and I in you, you will bear much <u>fruit</u>; apart from me you can do nothing.

CHAPTER 2

THE FRUIT OF LOVE

1. The fruit of love can be seen in how we treat people.
2. We have been commanded by God to bear the fruit of love.
3. Love helps all of the other fruit of the Spirit grow in our lives.
4. The original Greek word for love is *Agape,* and it means a caring and seeking for the highest good of another person without motive for personal gain.
5. *1 Corinthians 13:4-7 (NIV)*

   4 Love is patient and kind. It does not envy, it does not boast, it is not proud.

   5 It does not dishonor others, it is not self-seeking, it is not easily angered, and it keeps no record of wrongs.

   6 Love does not delight in evil but rejoices with the truth.

   7 It always protects, always trusts, always hopes, and always perseveres.
6. The four different words in Greek for love are:
   1) *Eros*
   2) *Storge*
   3) *Phileo*
   4) *Agape*
7. God showed and proved His love for us by the fact that while we were still sinners, Christ died for us.
8. The world will know that we are disciples of Christ if we love one another. *(John 13:35)*

9. *1 John 4:8 (KJV)* – He that loveth not knoweth not God; for <u>God is love.</u>

10. God is the Source of love.

CHAPTER 3

THE FRUIT OF JOY

1. Joy is a shout, a proclamation that can manifest in singing. Joy is defined as a triumph, a cheerful and calm delight. Joy is an inner rejoicing that abides despite outer circumstances.
2. False
3. The Lord is our <u>strength.</u>
4. True
5. Sixteen
6. Paul was in prison.
7. Happiness is external. Joy is internal. Happiness is based on feelings. Joy is based on knowledge. Happiness depends on what happens to us. Joy depends on who lives within us. Happiness is temporary. Joy is permanent. Happiness depends on outward circumstances. Joy depends on inward character. Happiness is based on chance. Joy is based on choice.
8. *Proverbs 17:22 (AMPC),* A happy heart is good <u>medicine</u> and a cheerful mind works healing, but a broken spirit dries up the bones.
9. *Romans 8:28 (NIV)* - And we know that in all things God works for the good of those who love him, who have been called <u>according to his purpose.</u>
10. Just by having a good attitude and being of good cheer, we bring <u>health</u> and <u>healing</u> to our bodies.

CHAPTER 4

THE FRUIT OF PEACE

1. *Webster's* Dictionary defines peace as a freedom from disquieting or oppressive thoughts or emotions.
2. Peace comes from a Greek word, which means <u>tranquility of mind.</u>
3. *Shalom*
4. *Shalom* means wholeness and completion–nothing missing, nothing lacking.
5. *Isaiah 26:3 (NKJV) says, "You will keep him in perfect peace, Whose mind is stayed on You, Because he trusts in You."*
6. We can keep our minds on Him by:
   ✓ Praising Him
   ✓ Praying to Him
   ✓ Speaking in agreement with God's Word
   ✓ Trusting Him
   ✓ Meditating on the Word of God
7. Whatever we focus on, we <u>magnify.</u>
8. According to *Psalm 29:11 (NIV)*, God blesses His people with peace
9. The three kinds of peace mentioned in chapter 4 are:
   1) Peace with God
   2) Peace with others
   3) Peace with yourself
10. According to *Isaiah 26:4 (AMPC)*, the Lord God is an Everlasting <u>Rock.</u>

CHAPTER 5

THE FRUIT OF PATIENCE

1. Patience is long-spirited, long-suffering with mildness, gentleness, moderation, and constancy.
2. *Proverbs 16:32 (AMPC), He who is slow to anger is better than the mighty, he who rules his [own] spirit than he who takes a city.*
3. Long-suffering
4. Long-suffering is the willingness to exercise patience, perseverance, and persistence in the pursuit of worthy goals.
5. The hardest thing for most Christians to do is to wait on the Lord.
6. Endurance, steadfastness, and patience.
7. *Ecclesiastes 7:8* tells us that the patient in spirit is better than the proud.
8. Two characteristics of being impatient are:
   1) Impatient people always try to avoid or eliminate discomfort or suffering.
   2) Impatient people cause stress, and stress can cause sickness.
9. Four great men in the Bible who waited patiently on the Lord are: Moses, Joseph, David, Abraham
10. What are three benefits of waiting on the Lord?

Waiting on the Lord:
   1) Builds hope
   2) Builds our faith
   3) Teaches us obedience

CHAPTER 6

THE FRUIT OF KINDNESS

1. Kindness is the ability to care for each other in the practical details of life.
2. Being kind to others is about <u>relationships.</u>
3. Success in Life + Failure at Relationships = <u>Failure.</u>
4. Three benefits of being kind are:
   1) When we are kind and friendly to others, the Bible says that we will have friends *(Proverbs 18:24 NKJV)*
   2) Sow kindness and you will reap kindness *(Galatians 6:7 NKJV)*
   3) We will have more joy and peace.
5. Ralph Waldo Emerson said:

   "You cannot do a kindness too soon, for you never know how soon it will be too late."

CHAPTER 7

THE FRUIT OF GOODNESS

1. Goodness is the moral quality, which constitute Christian excellence.
2. <u>God</u> is Good!
3. God wants to be good to <u>you.</u>
4. According to *Galatians 6:10 (NKJV)*, God wants us to do good to <u>all, especially to those who are of the household of faith.</u>
5. A simple act of kindness is a nice way to show goodness. Three simple acts of kindness are:

1) Giving a smile
2) Giving when you see a need
3) Giving someone a compliment

CHAPTER 8

THE FRUIT OF HUMILITY

1. Humility is freedom from pride and arrogance. It is a modest estimation of your own worth.
2. Humility also means <u>meekness</u>.
3. Meek means to be gentle or mild.
4. A meek man is a <u>powerful man</u>.
5. Pride is an unreasonable conceit of one's own superiority in talents, beauty, wealth, accomplishments, rank or elevation in office, which manifests itself in high-minded airs, distance from others, and often abuse of others.
6. *Proverbs 16:18 (AMPC)* – Pride goes before <u>destruction,</u> and a <u>haughty</u> spirit before a <u>fall</u>.
7. According to *Proverbs 15:33,* humility comes before honor.
8. Seven things God hate are:
   1) A proud look
   2) A lying tongue
   3) A hand that sheds innocent blood
   4) A heart that manufactures wicked thoughts and plans
   5) Feet that are swift in running to evil
   6) A false witness who breathes out lies
   7) He who sows discord among brethren
9. God wants us to humble ourselves under His mighty hand so He might exalt us in due time.
10. Pride can show up in our lives in the following ways:
    1) Perfectionism
    2) An inability to trust God

3) A need to control circumstances
4) A desire to impress people

CHAPTER 9

THE FRUIT OF FAITHFULNESS

1. Faithfulness means firm and unswerving loyalty and adherence to a person to whom one is united by promise, commitment, trustworthiness, and honesty.
2. In order for faith to develop and grow properly, we must *water* it with the Word of God.
3. Faith comes by hearing, and hearing by the Word of God.
4. *Luke 16:10 (NLT)* says that if you are faithful in little things, you will be faithful in <u>large ones</u>.
5. Promotion comes from God.
6. No
7. The fruit of the Spirit represents the character of God.
8. *Proverbs 27:6 (AMPC), Faithful are the wounds of a <u>friend</u>, but the <u>kisses</u> of an <u>enemy</u> are lavish and deceitful.*
9. We should do whatever we do on our jobs heartily (genuinely, wholeheartedly, sincerely), as to the Lord, and not unto men.
10. We should be faithful to:
    1) God
    2) Our spouse
    3) Our children
    4) Our friends
    5) Our church

CHAPTER 10

THE FRUIT OF SELF-CONTROL

1. Self-control means having control or mastery over one's own desires and passions.

   Self-control is restraint exercised over one's own impulse or emotions.

   Self-control is the art of controlling oneself.

2. It is so important for a leader to be self-controlled because the first person a leader leads is him or herself.

3. The day you become a leader, you lose the right to live selfishly.

4. *Proverbs 25:28 (NLT)* tells us that a person without self-control is like a city with broken-down walls.

5. Uncontrolled areas of your life that can harm your relationships are:

   1) Uncontrolled Anger
   2) Out of control spending
   3) Drinking too much
   4) Out of balanced ambition

6. Self-control is the difference between victory and defeat in the game of life.

7. Successful people control or manage their

   1) Time
   2) Tongue
   3) Emotions
   4) Finances

8. A quote by John Hancock Field states:

   "All worthwhile men have good thoughts, good ideas, and good

intentions, but precious few of them ever translate those into <u>*action.*</u>*"*

9. You should start small.
10. You become a great spiritual giant by spending a little time with God every day, and gradually increasing it.

ABOUT THE AUTHOR

MIRANDA BURNETTE is the president and founder of Miranda Burnette Ministries, Inc. S h e i s a licensed evangelist. She is also the founder of Keys to Success Academy, Inc., an online Leadership Bible School where she teaches people how to discover and fulfill their calling, to make their dreams a reality, to be successful in every area of their lives, and to be all God created them to be. The vision of Miranda Burnette Ministries is to educate, equip, and empower others to be successful leaders and reach their full God-given potential.

Miranda is the author of S*uccess Starts in Your Mind, Dare to Dream and Soar Like an Eagle, and Leader to Leader. S*he also makes an impact on the lives of others with her teachings on CD. She is the founder and president of I Can Christian Academy, Inc. Miranda and her husband, Morris, lives in Atlanta, Georgia and are the parents of two adult children, LaTrelle and Davin.

CONTACT INFORMATION

For more information or to order books contact:

Miranda Burnette Ministries, Inc.
P. O. Box 314
Clarkdale, GA 30111

E-mail
miranda@ mirandaburnetteministries.org

Website
www.mirandaburnetteministries.org

OTHER BOOKS BY MIRANDA BURNETTE

Dare to Dream and Soar Like an Eagle
The Sky is the Limit!

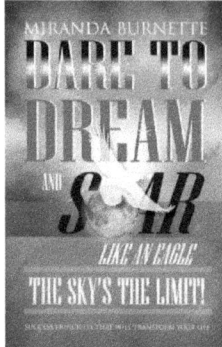

If you are ready to take the challenge to make your dreams a reality, this book is for you. In these pages, Miranda Burnette shares important success principles that will absolutely transform your life.

The keys contained in this powerful book will help you soar from level to level in order to fulfill God's purpose for your life.

Dare to Dream and Soar Like an Eagle will help you:

Maximize your potential

Achieve your goals

Clarify your vision

Cultivate inspired ideas

Release the seeds of greatness that God has placed inside you.

Recognize that God created you for *SUCCESS*

It doesn't matter who you are or what you are experiencing in your life right now, you have residing within you God-given ability to accomplish more than you could ever imagine. *So Dare to Dream and Soar Like an Eagle! The Sky's the Limit!*

Success Starts In Your Mind
A Manual on How to Think Your Way to Success

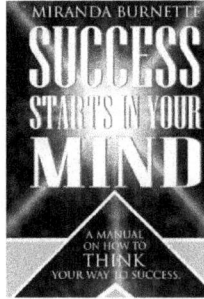

If you could change one thing in your life right now, what would you change?

Have you ever considered changing your thoughts? If you are frustrated, discontented, and disappointed with your life, if you want to be successful in different areas of your life, if you want to be freed from the bondage of bad habits, and if you want your life to change, *THIS BOOK IS FOR YOU!* If you want your life to change, you have to change your thinking. Your life won't change unless your thoughts change. You can change your life by changing your thoughts.

SUCCESS STARTS IN YOUR MIND will help you:

Understand the power of thoughts

Develop an understanding of the relationship between success and the mind

Think positively

Overcome the fear of success

Comprehend how what you think about yourself can dramatically affect your level of success

Realize that *Success Starts In Your Mind*

If you are not successful, or if you are not as successful as you would like to be, it is time for you to start *Thinking Your Way To Success.*

Leader to Leader

Inspiring Words for Women in Leadership

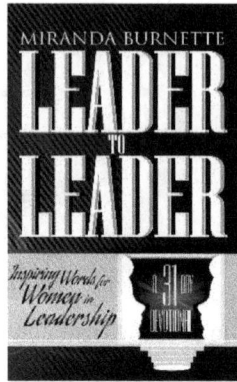

Do you want to be a strong, confident leader? Do you want to learn leadership principles that will take you and your organization to the next level? Do you desire to develop leaders, not just followers? Do you want to learn how to make good decisions? *THEN THIS BOOK IS FOR YOU*!

LEADER TO LEADER will help you to:

Discover how to be an effective leader

Develop principles of leadership that will help you be the leader others will follow

Learn the qualities of a great leader

Realize that failure is not fatal

Use your past mistakes as a stepping stone to rise to the next level

Lead by example

Develop great leaders

Read, study, and meditate on the leadership principles in this devotional and become the effective leader you've always wanted to be!